SOLDIERS INTO CAMP

The Battles at the Rosebud and the Little Bighorn

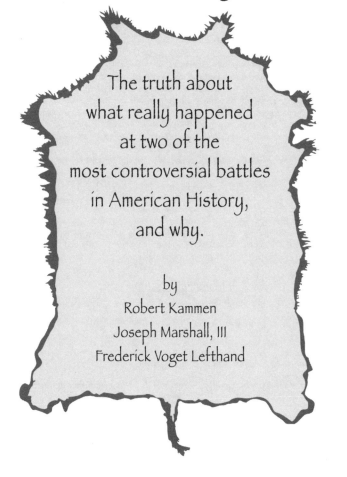

The truth about
what really happened
at two of the
most controversial battles
in American History,
and why.

by
Robert Kammen
Joseph Marshall, III
Frederick Voget Lefthand

Cloud Peak Publishing, Inc.
4801 Lang NE, Suite 110
Albuquerque, New Mexico 87109
(505) 833-4000
Printed in the United States of America

Published by: Cloud Peak Publishing, Inc.
http://www.cloudpeakpublishing.com

Managing Editor: Paul Harwitz

Soldiers Falling Into Camp

This new (2nd) edition, revised, corrected, & augmented,
published by Cloud Peak Publishing, Inc.

ISBN 10: 0-9779039-0-7
ISBN 13: 978-0-9779039-0-0
(Replaces previous ISBN: 1-879915-04-9) Former publisher defunct.
Library of Congress Control Number: 2006928624

Printed and Bound in the United States of America
This Book is Printed on Acid-Free Paper.

Active print edition: 10 9 8 7 6 5 4 3
Standard Address Number: SAN 8 5 0 - 5 4 3 8

This work is dedicated to the memory of the Lakota and Cheyenne warriors who fought courageously at the battles of the Rosebud and Greasy Grass Rivers in June of 1876.

Many of their names are lost to history, but their collective deeds in the defense of their families, their lands, and their way of life should never be forgotten.

Hokahe!

Sitting Bull.
Photo courtesy of the Library of Congress.
Credit: D. F. Barry, 1885.

Table of Contents

Photo courtesy of the Library of Congress.
CREDIT: "Portrait of Major General (as of Apr. 15, 1865)
George A. Custer, Officer of the Federal Army."
Between 1860 & 1865.

To the Reader

The Battle of the Little Big Horn continues to arouse curiosity and ignite imagination. It has created heroes and villains. Perhaps it has even made heroes of those who really were villains, and villains of those who really were heroes. In any case, the Battle and those who fought it will always own a certain mystique and will always stay behind a thin veil of mystery.

It was called the Greasy Grass Fight by the Lakota , and it is the most glaring symbol of the clash of cultures on the High Plains in the 19th Century. But that grandiose description overshadows the fact that it was a human event. It was instigated by human attitudes, thoughts, actions, and reactions. Human beings, people, were on both sides of that fateful struggle. It is a fact too often ignored, and to ignore it distorts the telling of the story.

Another aspect of the Greasy Grass story also often overlooked is the Battle of the Rosebud, eight days earlier and some thirty miles to the south. There the Lakota and Cheyenne faced a larger force commanded by General George Crook and fought them to a standstill. A victory, for all intents and purposes, for the Lakota and their Cheyenne allies. One which effectively eliminated Crook from that summer's grand plan to catch the Lakota in a three-way pincer movement. And, perhaps more importantly, their victory over Crook was the best rehearsal possible for the Lakota and Cheyenne. It prepared them for what was to come eight days later.

We do not purport to tell herein the ultimate and "once and for all" story of the Greasy Grass Fight. What we have tried to do is tell a story of a human event. We have based it on facts available in written form as well as information handed down through Lakota and Crow oral traditions.

Robert Kammen
Frederick Lefthand
Joseph Marshall

A Glossary of Terms

Arikara - a northern plains tribe living on the upper reaches of the Missouri river.

Ash Creek - a tributary flowing into the Greasy Grass. Now known as Reno Creek.

Blackfeet - a northern plains tribe of northwestern Montana.

Crow - also known as Absaroka, living in the south-central Montana and north central Wyoming.

Dakota - The Eastern Sioux, one of two groups living primarily east of the Missouri River. The eastern or D dialect of the parent language.

Greasy Grass River - known as the Little Bighorn to the Whites.

Hunkpapa - *Those who camp by the end of the entrance.* A division of the Lakota

Isanti - *Those who make knives.* Another name for the Dakota or eastern Sioux. They are made up of four divisions.

Itazipacola - *Those without bows.* A division of the Lakota.

Lakota - The Western Sioux, living primarily west of the Missouri River. The western or L dialect of the parent language.*

Mahpiya Luta - *Red Cloud.* Oglala Lakota.

Medicine Tail Creek - a tributary flowing into the Greasy Grass. Now known as Medicine Tail Coulee.

Miniconju - *Those who plant by the water.* A division of the Lakota.

Nakota - The Central Sioux, one of the two groups living primarily east of the Missouri River. The central or N dialect of the parent language.*

Oglala - *To scatter one's own.* A division of the Lakota.

Oohenunpa - *Two boilings or two kettles.* A division of the Lakota.

Paha Sapa – The sacred center of the Lakota Nation. Referred to by whites as the Black Hills.

Pawnee - a southern plains tribe living in the south-central area of what is now Nebraska.

Pizi - *Gall*. Hunkpapa Lakota.

Sahiyela - The Lakota word for *Cheyenne*. The Cheyenne word for themselves is *Tsistsistas*.

Shining Mountains - known as the Big Horn Mountains to the Crow and whites.

Sicangu - *Burnt Thigh*. A division of the Lakota. Called Brule by the French.

Sihasapa - *Blackfeet or black sole*. Formerly a division of the Lakota. Sometimes referred to as Rocky Mountain Sioux. Not to be confused with the Blackfeet or Blackfoot Tribe of Montana.

Sioux - Derived from the Ojibwa (Chippewa) Indian word *naddewasioux*, and shortened to its present form. Sioux is presently applied to all bands and linguistic groups of the Lakota, Nakota, and Dakota.

Travois – A sledge made of two poles which support a cloth, hide, or net, used to transport items and drawn by a horse. Before the arrival of the horse, one or more dogs were used to pull it. The word is French-Canadian in origin. The plural can be travois or travoises.

Tasunke Witko - *Crazy Horse*. (More properly translated as His Crazy Horse.) Oglala Lakota.

Tatunka Iyotake - *Sitting Bull*. Hunkpapa Lakota.

The-People-Who-Live-In-Earth-Lodges—Mandans. Only occasionally in conflict with the Lakota. Their numbers were greatly reduced by a smallpox epidemic in the 1830s.

Wickiup – A hut made of an oval-shaped framed covered with branches, brush, grass, etc. There are also other spellings.

*Lakota, Nakota, and Dakota mean *"allies"* or *"an alliance of friends."* The names for months were based on occurrences in nature consistent with the time of year or the weather. The names were not standardized or universal. Different groups of the Sioux often used different names for the same months. Months were the cycles of the moon.

Moon of Frost in the Lodge. Tioheyunka Wi. January.

Moon of Popping Trees. Cannanpopa Wi. February.

Moon of Snowblindness. Istawicayazanpi Wi. March.

Moon when Geese Return. Magaglihunnipi Wi. April.

Moon of Shedding Ponies. Pehingnunipi Wi. May.

Moon of Ripening Berries. Wipazuka Waste Wi. June.

The Middle Moon. Wicokannanji. July.

In the ancient annual calendar, there were thirteen moons, or months, because of thirteen lunar cycles. *The Middle Moon,* now called July, was so entitled because it had six moons preceding it and six moons following it.

Moon When All Things Ripen. Wasutun Wi. August.

Moon When Leaves Turn Brown. Canapegi Wi. September.

Moon When Leaves Fall. Canapekasna Wi. October.

Winter Moon. Waniyetu Wi. November

The Mid-Winter Moon. Wanicokan Wi. December.

One of the winter months was called Wiotehika, or *"Moon of the Terrible"* or *"Moon of Hard Times."* It was the winter month when conditions were the harshest. When the Sioux began to use the modern non-Indian calendar, they dropped a month from their ancient way of naming the months, or moons. *The Moon of the Terrible* is often left off the modern calendar.

Sitting Bull's Family.
Portrait of Sitting Bull, his mother and his daughter holding child.
Photo courtesy of the Library of Congress.
Photograph by Miller.

General George Crook ("Three Stars")
Courtesy of the Denver Public Library, Western History Collection,
Photographer: D. F. Barry, 1889,
Call Number: B-936.

CHAPTER 1

The Battle of the Rosebud

It was evening, in the Moon of the Ripening Cherries, and the Lakota encampment near Ash Creek was shedding the bustle of the day and settling down as darkness approached. Ash Creek flowed into Greasy Grass River, known as Little Big Horn to the whites in their year of 1876. The camp had been growing since word had spread across Lakota territory there was a new leader of all the Lakota. Many left their reservations to follow this new leader, hoping that he would bring an end to the white man's encroachment into Lakota country. Earlier, in the Moon of Snowblindness, soldiers from Three Stars' army had attacked He Dog's camp on the Little Powder River. Though the Lakota had retaliated and beat back the soldiers some days later, the boldness of the attack fit in with the message sent by the chief of all whites from Washington. After the Moon of Frost in the Lodge, January, any Lakota not found on a reservation, he had said, would be considered "hostile." "Hostiles" could be shot on sight by the soldiers. Clearly, the new leader of the Lakota had a heavy burden to bear. And on this particular evening, scouts had ridden from the south with more news of Three Stars, General George Crook.

It was a good time and a bad time for the people in the large and ever-growing encampment. It was good to visit, to see relatives and old friends, and to know that the Lakota were still a strong people. But the news carried by the scouts about Three Stars was a reminder of how life was changing. Eight winters past, the Oglala Lakota had forced the soldiers to leave their fort along Piney Creek, and had burned it to the ground. Now Three Stars was in that same country, at the foot of the Shining Mountains, and moving his soldiers north. North. Perhaps toward this camp. Something had to be done.

Though there was no outright fear that Three Stars would reach them soon, there was uncertainty because the soldiers had been getting bolder. But some of the old people reminded others of the Hunkpapa medicine-man's vision. Only days ago, during the Sun Dance, Sitting Bull was given a vision. A vision of many bluecoat soldiers falling into a great Lakota encampment. "We know what will happen if Three Stars came here," some said, referring to Sitting Bull's vision. But others still worried. Even though Sitting Bull was powerful and his vision was not to be taken lightly, and even though there were nearly a thousand Lakota and Cheyenne warriors in camp, there was still worry. The white men were persistent, and did not keep their promises. They had promised to let the Lakota live on their own lands in peace, if the whites could put a road through it. The Lakota were not left to live in peace, especially after the white man's precious gold had been found in the Paha Sapa. Now the chief of all whites wanted the Lakota to live on reservations, to give up the old hunting life. That was like asking bear and elk to fly, or the eagle and the hawk to grow hooves and teeth. Better to die a free hunter and warrior, some thought. And perhaps that was coming.

Messengers were sent to all the camp circles on this warm

evening. There was still a strong light in the west when all the leaders gathered in the great council lodge. There the scouts told their news.

To the south, Three Stars had been joined by many Snakes and Crows, old enemies of the Lakota and Cheyenne. Now the whole force had left their camp on Goose Creek and was moving north. They had marched past the Tongue River and were just south of Rosebud Creek when the scouts last saw them. A good day's ride from the Lakota encampment. Too close. Something had to be done about Three Stars.

Many people gathered outside the council lodge to listen. Inside the lodge, some advised caution and some were in favor of immediate attack. There was much debate back and forth. The young warriors waiting outside were hot to ride against Three Stars. There was little agreement, until one man rose to speak. The quiet one. The new leader of them all. The one whose very name evoked fear from his enemies, awe from his own people, and jealousy from those who wished for his status. Crazy Horse.

"My relatives," he said. "The bluecoat soldiers are different from us. That we know. They fight, but I think they are not warriors. They fight because it is their work. They are paid to do so. The Lakota warrior fights to protect his people, his family, and the good ways of people." He paused as murmurs of agreement went through the council lodge. "It is time to put an end to the white man in our land. It is time to finish this thing. I will ride against Three Stars. Those who wish can come with me. But let us not forget the helpless ones. I think it would be good if some older warriors could stay to protect them. It is a sacred duty best left to those with many battles."

Shouts of approval rang through the evening air. Runners hurried to all parts of the great camp. Crazy Horse would lead all who would follow against Three Stars and his soldiers.

Children watched the sudden activity with wide eyes, not fully understanding its meaning. Older boys looked longingly at the warriors, hoping to be asked to go along. Wives and mothers were at once fearful and proud, but mostly keeping their feelings to themselves as they helped their warriors prepare. Some of the very old women stood outside their lodges and began to sing the strongheart songs. Old men quickly gave advice to a son or a grandson, and secretly wished for the strength of their youth so they could ride into battle again. But in the end they too gathered their weapons, satisfied to be the protectors of the village and determined that no white enemy would enter its circle without paying a fearful price.

In the Oglala camp, a woman worked in her lodge to get things ready for her warrior husband. On a painted deer hide just outside the lodgeflap she placed his bow in its case and a quiver with over thirty arrows, a stone war club, a paint bag, a smaller bag with medicine objects of his vision, a shield made of seven thicknesses of buffalo hide, a lance wrapped in red with four eagle feathers tied to it, and a rifle in an elk hide sheath with a bullet bag. Soon he came and she helped him pack. Whatever he would not carry was loaded onto the tan and white mare. His favorite war horse. The second war horse, a bay gelding, would be on a lead.

For a few heartbeats, the slender, light-haired warrior held his wife within the folds of his blanket, and then swung onto the mare. Black Shawl sent up a prayer as she watched her warrior ride away, bow and arrows on his back, shield on his left arm, the rifle across the withers of the horse, and the bay on a short lead. The lance he left behind, stuck end first into the ground with its glistening point toward the sky. Black Shawl watched her husband, the Oglala war leader, ride away into the fading evening light.

Not long after Crazy Horse's quiet call to arms, nearly a thousand warriors joined him on the edge of the encampment. Most of them were Lakota, but there were a good number of Cheyenne, too. Many were already painted for battle and all were equipped to fight. Some, like Crazy Horse, rode one war horse and lead a second.

Women sang the strongheart songs as the great thongs of warriors circled the camp. Lances decorated with eagle feathers and rifle barrels silhouetted against the darkening sky. Quivers bristled with arrows, war clubs dangled from quilled or beaded belts. Horses bobbed their heads and pranced, sensing the mood of their riders. Drums rang like thunder, as even the very old ones among the watching crowds had a difficult time remembering when last they had seen such a thing. The warriors completed their circling of the great camp and rode into the night. They rode toward Three Stars and his Snake and Crow allies, and overhead, above the tall lodgepoles decorated with streaming banners and a few scalp locks, the nighthawks soared and dived after fleeing insects.

They rode in several long files behind the warriors who knew the trails and could find their way easily in the dark. No one spoke, although no command had been passed forbidding it. Each warrior knew what was expected of him. It was knowledge learned and gained individually but used for the good of all. That was the way of the Lakota warrior, passed from one generation to the next since a time past the remembering of even the oldest man in the encampment. If there was a word to be spoken, it passed from one man to the next, softly, so as not to be heard above the hoofbeats.

Sometimes in the night, Crazy Horse signaled a short rest. Nearly every warrior slid from his horse's back. Some drank a little from their water flasks or took a mouthful or two of dried meat. Except for a soft nicker or a stamping of a hoof, there was silence. Next to one another, silence was there best ally. In a short while, a low soft whistle signaled all to start once again.

Just before dawn, the war leader called another halt. Another rest and time to make final preparations. Preparations for battle, and for a warrior's death should it come. In the dim but growing light warriors adorned themselves with their medicine things, or counted bullets for the few rifles among them. Many strung their bows and tied quivers to the front at the beltline so arrows could be in easy reach. Crazy Horse untied his hair and put on a calf hide cape, then dismounted and threw gopher dust over his horses. He believed that the gopher was best at hiding in and on the Earth. So he always borrowed a little of the power from that small being to help him on the hunt and in battle. Then he sent out word asking the leaders of different warrior groups to join him for a little planning.

In the still dim light of dawn, a group of warriors stood as shadowy shapes around Crazy Horse. A small group of scouts had been sent ahead to learn the exact location of Three Stars' night camp, and to find the Lakota scouts who had stayed behind from two days past. "I think we will meet many soldiers," Crazy Horse told the circle of warrior leaders. "I know they all have fast shooting rifles, many more than we have. And each soldier has many bullets. So our warriors must attack in strong waves, like the wasp and sting like he does. We must try to push close enough for those who have only the bow." He paused to glance ever so briefly at each strong face. There was no fear here. Only purpose. "We must fight," he went on, "as we always have, as we have been taught. Like the wasp who attacks in deadly way. Like the wolf who defends his home, no matter the size or number of his enemies, and never gives in. Remember the helpless ones. Remember that we are warriors and that this is the way each of us has chosen. Remember that we do this so the people may live."

A distant shout and shots came from just the other side of a ridge to the south. It had begun. *"Hokahe!"* yelled Crazy Horse. "Do not be afraid! It is a good day to die!"

The scouts sent ahead had run into a group of Crows riding up the slope. A Crow fired first and wounded a Lakota. Return-fire knocked two Crows from their horses. The Lakota warriors waiting behind the ridge rode quickly to the top. Below them a few Crows were retreating toward the valley floor at a full gallop. And the valley was full of soldiers. They were on both sides of the creek and up the slope of the ridge on the far side. The fleeing Crows alerted all the soldiers.

A bugle blared. Thin piercing notes into the warm air, almost like a mourning cry. In a little while most of the soldiers were organized. The horse soldiers caught and mounted their horses. Walking soldiers moved into tight bunches and began moving toward the Lakota. There was already much dust in the air.

Crazy Horse held back the warriors, waiting for the soldiers to stretch themselves out as they moved up the ridge. But the soldiers' rifle fire was getting close, hitting the dirt near the horses' hooves or sniping past a warrior's head in a high-pitched angry whine. The warriors fell back to another ridge. A wave of horse soldiers dismounted and joined the walking soldiers. Many were crawling from rock to rock, scattering themselves just as Crazy Horse hoped they would. He did not pass up the opening.

Crazy Horse signaled the warriors closest to him and led a furious charge down the slope toward the soldiers on foot. Soldiers went down. Many moved back down the slope, hard pressed by the sudden Lakota charge. Several warriors to the right of Crazy Horse rode in close enough to hit a few soldiers with arrows before they turned their horses back up the slope. It was the first of many brave things the Oglala war leader saw that day.

A new wave of soldiers joined the fight, coming from across the creek. Behind them, riding hard, came a large bunch of Snakes. They moved to one side of the charging soldiers and left them behind. They came in so close that it was difficult to tell a Lakota from a Snake inside the smoke and dust. Better to withdraw, since it was hard to tell friend from enemy with the Snakes in so close.

Gunfire, smoke, and dust began to fill the valley of the Rosebud. The fighting was beginning to spread out over many ridges and slopes. A warrior named Good Weasel rode up to tell Crazy Horse that. He told of how fast one Lakota charge managed to slice a bluecoat column in two. Then the soldiers regrouped and charged the Lakota, nearly managing to put them in a crossfire. But the Lakota slipped out of the trap with only a few men wounded. Then Good Weasel said, "My friend, our people need to see where you are. I have brought a cousin to ride at your side and carry the eagle feather banner. It is the old way. And the warriors, especially the younger ones, can know where you are. It will give them courage."

Crazy Horse nodded silently. Good Weasel motioned and a slender young warrior on a black horse rode forward. In his hand was the red-wrapped staff of the war leader, on which were tied many, many eagle feathers. "My friend," Crazy Horse said to the young warrior, "I am honored that you will ride with me."

The young warrior shook his head. "No, Uncle," he replied, "the honor is mine."

Crazy Horse and his standard-bearer rode off to the south, to see how the battle was going. Screams of horses and shouts of soldiers could be heard thinly. They saw a large group of soldiers on a bluff, soldiers who were hard-pressed to keep their position in the face of sharp and relentless attacks. On the other side of the creek another large group of soldiers were firing from a hill. They were assaulted from the south and southwest at the same time by two strong charges, one Cheyenne and one Lakota. The soldiers could not hold the hill and moved down the northwest slope, back toward another group of soldiers. Behind them the Cheyenne and Lakota were picking up their own wounded and carrying them far away from the fighting. But horses were stumbling now, weak and tired.

An Oglala rode up to tell Crazy Horse that more Hunkpapa had just now arrived and were joining in. Good, thought Crazy Horse, fresh horses and more precious bullets. He moved back toward the north, behind a sheltering knoll. There he switched horses to let the tired mare rest. The bay was anxious, hot for the fight.

On his way to join the Hunkpapa, Crazy Horse watched the Cheyenne war leader Comes In Sight have his horse shot from under him. He fell between two small groups of soldiers shooting from the cover of willows. They began to encircle him. A rider, unmistakably a woman, broke from the Cheyenne lines and rode to the Cheyenne warrior, now fighting on foot. Through the bullets she rode and slowed just enough to allow the Cheyenne to jump up behind her. They rode to safety, back and forth among the soldier bullets. From far hillsides Lakota and Cheyenne warriors lifted shouts to acknowledge the courage of the woman who was a warrior.

Crazy Horse fought alongside the Hunkpapa for a time. He and the young standard-bearer crawled within rifle range of soldiers far to the north of the main body. If there was such a thing. There was much confusion among the bluecoats. Several large groups of them were scattered throughout the little valley of the Rosebud. But owing to their numbers, more than the Lakota and Cheyenne together, they were holding their own. A time or two they even charged the Lakota.

Good Weasel once again found Crazy Horse. " We are being pushed back," he said, motioning to an area where the gunfire was heavy. "If we break, I think it could be very bad for us." Crazy Horse and his young companion ran back to their horses and followed Good Weasel. They topped a small hill in time to see a group of Lakota galloping away from the fight. On the fresh bay, Crazy Horse caught up quickly, shouting as he rode among them. "Death is not the enemy! Do not fear it! IF we are to die, let us do so with our faces toward the real enemy! The soldiers are that way!" he yelled, pointing back over his shoulder.

The warriors turned.

Turning the bay, Crazy Horse put him into a gallop toward the soldiers. The young warrior with the eagle feather staff caught up, working his horse hard. Hundreds of hooves pounded like thunder from a sudden summer storm, and moved just as swiftly. Arrows and bullets rained down on the soldiers' positions. The warriors who had been retreating only a short time before were now sweeping hard into their enemy, a flood the soldiers could not turn back. The Crows and Snakes were the first to break and gallop away. It turned into the kind of close-in fighting the Lakota liked best. Soldiers were trampled beneath the hooves of flying war horses or knocked from their saddles with a skillful swing of the war club. Here and there a warrior stopped his charge long enough to recover a soldier's rifle, dropped from dead hands or thrown away in fear.

The strength of the charge carried the soldiers and the pursuing Lakota down into the little valley. Here the soldiers scattered. Some seeking cover anywhere they could. Others managed to rejoin Three Stars' main group. There they reformed and deployed to turn back the Lakota assault.

Crazy Horse signaled a return back across the creek and led the main group of warriors north, toward a curve in Rosebud Creek where the small valley was narrow. He sent word back to the other groups of warriors that the soldiers and their Crow and Snake allies might try to follow them into the narrow place. A good place for an ambush.

He passed the word among the warriors following him. It would be good to let the horses walk, to rest them and let the soldiers think they were quitting the fight. He and the young standard-bearer turned back to see if the ruse would fool the soldiers. It did. A long string of horse soldiers were coming hard. By the time they reached the narrow spot, the Lakota would be in place and waiting. But before the trap could be sprung, the Crows rode up fast to stop the soldiers' pursuit. The soldiers turned and rode back south. Crazy Horse heard fast rifle-fire after that, but he was certain the fight was over. He sent four messengers back into the valley to tell the warriors still there to pull out. It was time to go home.

The sun was well into the afternoon half of the sky when the Lakota and Cheyenne broke off the fight. A rear-guard rode far behind to keep an eye on Three Stars. Toward evening the main body stopped to rest. To Crazy Horse's surprise, the young standard-bearer fell from his horse. He dismounted and went to the young man, and saw the gunshot wound in the young warrior's side.

After drag-poles were prepared to carry the dead and wounded, the warriors resumed their homeward trek. Night found them still on the trail, moving slowly. They had ridden to battle in the friendly folds of darkness. On their return, they hid once again in its comforting embrace. Messengers were sent ahead to alert the encampment and to carry the news of victory, and of those dead and wounded.

It was the old way, a good way for warriors to return to camp. And though this was a victory ride, the warriors rode quietly. Talking softly if they talked at all. Thinking of the battle. It had been a hard fight. One to stop a bad enemy. A fight that took away some good men from their families and wounded many more.

The first faint glow of new daylight rimmed the eastern horizon when some of the scouts caught up. They reported that Three Stars had lost over fifty soldiers dead or badly wounded. He was burying his dead in the dark, the scouts said.

The great encampment was fully awake at dawn, waiting to care for the returning warriors. Though there was an air of celebration, many people kept their silence for those families who were already mourning their dead. Before Crazy Horse returned to his own lodge, he first went to eight other lodges. At each he quietly thanked the relatives for the life their warrior had given for the people.

Finally, he stopped at the lodge of Black Wolf, the young warrior who had carried the staff of the war-leader. Crazy Horse told the young man's family of his conduct, even as a grandmother tended to the young man's wound. "I am honored to have ridden with you, Uncle," said young Black Wolf. Crazy Horse shook his head.

"No," he replied, "the honor is mine."

At his own lodge he saw the lance still standing as he had left it. Black Shawl had a meal ready. She could see the weariness in him as he moved to the back of the lodge. He took the bowl of soup, savoring the good smell from the meat, turnips, and onions.

"How did you know I was thinking of this good soup?" he asked her quietly. She smiled and went to bring his things into the lodge.

"A wind came up strong yesterday," she told him. "It blew over many meat racks. But your lance stood good and strong. That is how I know you would come home victorious. The wind could not blow over your lance."

Crazy Horse nodded, a light in his tired eyes. "When the hearts of our women are strong," he said, "our warriors can be no less."

Two days after the Rosebud fight, the Oglala war-leader sat alone on a hill to the east of the encampment. There had been talk of moving since the horse herds were quickly eating down the grass. But that was small thing to worry over. Camps could be moved rapidly and skillfully. When it was time, it would be done. A greater worry was the bluecoat soldiers, and all of the other whites, for that matter.

There seemed to be no good answer to the problem of the whites. Since before the Fort Laramie councils, the first when he was but a boy, the whites had been a problem. Their actions and their thinking regarding the Lakota were clearly those of a people who thought themselves better. Even one of their holy men said that the Great Spirit was a false god, and that their God was the only true and all-powerful one. How could there be peace with such a people? A people who behaved in peace as they did in war. A people who took as if everything belonged to them in the first place. A people who were like the prairie tornado, approaching with a heavy promise of fury and turmoil. All of that held very little good for the Lakota. Unless there was a turning point.

Crazy Horse looked up to see a red-backed hawk swoop down toward the prairie. But if the winged hawk was after anything in particular, he came up with nothing. Perhaps it was a sign, the warrior thought. But if so, then for who? For the Lakota, or for the bluecoats?

The empty talons of the departing hawk brought another

thing to mind. Many days before the Rosebud fight, the great Hunkpapa medicine-man, Sitting Bull, had a stirring vision. A vision from the Sun Dance. A vision of many soldiers coming into the great Lakota camp, and dying. Many soldiers falling into camp.

Crazy Horse was certain the vision had helped push the Lakota and Cheyenne to victory against Three Stars. But, still, it was not the victory in the vision of Sitting Bull. No soldiers came near the great encampment. The Lakota had taken the fight to the soldiers. Was Sitting Bull's vision yet to come about? Yes. Of that, the Oglala was certain.

But a vision alone was not enough to assure victory, Crazy Horse thought. Soldiers falling into camp was only part of what could happen. He was certain of that, too. It was that yet unseen, an unknown which must not be taken lightly. Soldiers falling into camp could happen at a great cost. Another victory was to come, but the price of it was one of those unknown things. For everything gained, something was lost. Eight good men dead and many others wounded was the price of victory over Three Stars. What would be the price of many soldiers falling into camp? Crazy Horse wondered.

He returned to the camp to hear the news of Three Stars moving back south, back toward Goose Creek. Then came more news of soldier movements far to the north along the Yellowstone River. He considered these things as he walked to his lodge. To the west a dark line of clouds sat on the horizon like warriors bunching for a charge. He wondered when the storm would hit the great encampment. Perhaps, he thought, the storm would wait until the camp moved northward to the banks of Greasy Grass. The Little Bighorn, as whites called it.

Four of Custer's Crow scouts at the battlefield. (1880 – 1900)
White Man Runs Him, Hairy Moccasin, Curly, and Goes Ahead.
Photo courtesy of the Denver Public Library, Western History Collection,
Call Number: X-31275.

Curly was a 17-year-old Crow scout who rode with the Seventh Cavalry
led by Lt. Col. George Custer in 1876.
Courtesy of the Denver Public Library, Western History Collection,
photo by D. F. Barry (1882),
Call Number: B-172

CHAPTER 2

Curly: A 17-Year-Old Crow Scout

Saturday - June 24, 1876

Down the Valley of Rosebud

He was seventeen, and he was afraid of what lay ahead in the tangled darkness gripping the valley floor.

A heartbeat later there came the eerie rippling sound of an arrow hawk diving onto its prey, and his dappled horse pirouetted around in a tight circle. Quickly he brought his horse under control, as his companion said, "Perhaps the Sioux sent that as a warning . . . "

By starlight he could see the hard set to Hairy Moccasin's face framed by the coif of long black hair, the dark intensity in the eyes. He, Curly, a Crow scout, felt a surge of reassurance.

He said quietly, "That sound pierced my heart to chase my fear away."

He was darkly handsome, with chiseled features, and tall as were many Crow. Burnished black hair hung over his shoulders. Like the other Crow scout, he cradled his rifle in his arm. His other

17

weapon, a bow and quiver, slung across his back. They were naked but for loincloths, moccasins, eagle feathers thrust in their hair.

They had been out since eleven this evening, according to Lieutenant Varnum's big turnip-shaped watch. But a curt order from the commander of the 7th Cavalry had held Varnum with the main column, at least ten miles further to the north and bedded down for the night.

Across Rosebud Creek were the vague shadows of four more Crow scouts ghosting their horses to the south, while the Arikara scouts, guides Mitch Bouyer, a half-blood, and Lonesome Charlie Reynolds, were fanned out toward the valley walls but holding back a little to let the Crow bear the brunt of any ambush.

Eastward the pall of the night was slowly lifting, a palish gray tinting the sky just above the horizon, with ground objects just beginning to emerge out of the blackness. Hours ago, or so it seemed to Curly, the moon had gone behind the Little Wolf Mountains. They were holding to a walk, now following the creek bending southwesterly, a narrow ribbon of water still swollen with spring runoff. In passing through shrubbery, the thin, limber branches quivered slightly before stilling again, as there was no wind.

Here they could see a long way down the valley. Ever since early yesterday, the 23rd of June, they'd had little difficulty following the wide swath of trail left by the Lakota. They did so now, lowering their eyes to the scattering of debris left behind, like a small pile of bones, some of the bones split open to get at the marrow. Even in walking dust spurted out from under the unshod hooves of their mounts passing over ground that appeared as if it had been plowed up, which it had been by a horse herd the Crow scouts tallied to be in the thousands, and raked by hundreds of lodge poles, this huge body of horse and Lakota heading upstream.

At times they'd pause to examine the bones in order to discover when the Lakota had passed through, no longer than two days ago. Or feel the earth under the fire spots, or look at beetle-

18

worked horse droppings. From all of this they knew the Lakota encampment contained all of the seven tribes of the Teton Lakota, the Cheyenne, and lesser tribes. Far too formidable a force for Yellow Hair's pony soldiers.

Hairy Moccasin reined up. "The grass is chewed to the roots. . . here in the Rosebud . . . and even on the hills outside the valley. It is as if locusts had passed through."

"You said they would head west . . ."

"Toward the Ashaikata, the Little Big Horn."

The yip-yapping of a coyote brought Curly's eyes away for a moment, then he said, "Our enemy the Lakota know the soldiers are coming ..." He nudged his horse after Hairy Moccasin.

"Only because our people got word to them."

"They come and steal our horses, our women, as we do theirs. Our chiefs say this has to do with our land. Still , I ..."

"Someday this will be revealed to you." He gestured at something that had emerged from the fabric of night. "What do you make of that?" As he spurred his horse into a canter, Hairy Moccasin cupped a hand to h is mouth, the lonely call of a loon taking wing across the creek.

Now they passed over encirclements in the loamy earth telling where lodges had stood, and further on there was another ring, and still another. This was just one of the places the Lakota had stopped to make camp, and they knew the encampment would stretch on for three, four miles. Now it was the skeletal frame of a large circular Sun Dance arbor that found them reining up their horses. Scattered around the arbor were other branch affairs slightly larger than wickiups, and he murmured to Curly, "Sweat lodges. It seems our enemy the Lakota seeks guidance from the Great Spirit."

Creekward came the sound of horses splashing across and toward them, and they swung down, with Hairy Moccasin handing his reins to Curly. He told the younger scout to tarry there as he

19

hefted his Winchester. He was the smallest and most alert of the Crows, in his early thirties, with piercing black eyes. He padded silently over to the Sun Dance arbor.

Easing inside, Hairy Moccasin found the pine boughs were brittle to the touch. The center pole was still up, with tatters fastened to it at the top where the buffalo image and other ceremonial objects had hung. As he took this in, from outside came the hoot-hooting of an owl, which was a signal for the rest of the scouts to come in. Lowering his glance, he saw the stick thrust in the ground, to which was attached the dried scalp of a white man. To his face there came a pondering grimace. Yellow Hair has lost no men? He grasped his hunting knife and stooped to cut the scalp away from the stick, and now he slipped outside to rejoin the others.

In approaching the four other scouts standing by Curly he held out his trophy, but it seemed Goes Ahead had more important news, as he said, "Over there, on a sand-bar, we found pictures drawn with a stick. They say an army is coming . . ."

"A warning to other tribes on their way to join the Lakota. This Sun Dance arbor — it is the work of Sitting Bull." White Man Runs Him, now that he had their undivided attention, added, "Because I have heard Sitting Bull is seeking a vision. These sweat lodges, perhaps they will tell us something?"

Drifting in from both sides of the creek were the Arikara scouts, counting among their number the Negro Isaiah Dorman, known as *wasicun sapa* or the black white man. Further out came the half-blood Bouyer and Lonesome Charlie.

It was some of the Arikara clustering in to follow the Crow scouts moving over to take in a sweat lodge that had been torn down. One of the Arikara, Stabbed, who was a medicine-man, shouldered his horse in even closer. What he viewed with the others were a few stones that had been fire-heated and then doused with water. Afterwards they had been adorned with pictures, on one side shod hoof prints, meaning horse soldiers, on the other side pony tracks of the Lakota. Between these rows of stones and etched in the hard-packed ground were figures representing dead men, their heads toward the tracks of the Indians.

Fear gaped Stabbed's eyes as he intoned, "This is strong medicine!" Now he took notice of the scalp held by Hairy Moccasin, and then Curly called to them from where he'd gone to study the remains of another sweat lodge.

"What do you make of this?"

Everyone swung to move that way, as did Buffalo Ancestor, one of a handful of Sioux scouts, the others holding back on their horses in a stoical silence. A gesture from Curly brought all eyes to the floor of the sweat lodge and to three stones painted red and set in a row while false dawn had set in to reveal the flickering of emotions playing on their faces, uncertainty, fear, anger.

The Arikara, Stabbed, or "Ree", as they were known to the other Plains Indians, began chanting as he wheeled his horse away. He brought the other Arikara scouts away from this spiritual place of the Lakota and to a copse of trees.

Soon the death chant of the Arikara scouts brought a reddish tint to the eastern sky.

At the sweat lodge Buffalo Ancestor said gravely as he gazed around, "The Great Powers have promised the Lakota a great victory ... and if the whites do not come to them ... the Lakota will search the horse soldiers out."

"Sitting Bull ."

Everyone looked at White Man Runs Him.

"This is his vision."

Just back of the Indians pressing around the sweat lodge stood Reynolds, and alongside the guide from Kentucky, and Custer's favorite scout, the Arikara, Bloody Knife. Hovering near-by were Mitch Bouyer and Dorman. Reynolds refrained from speaking until those by the sweat lodge turned his way.

Then he said quietly, "Bloody Knife, here, tells me the Arikara scouts are going to hold here until the Regiment arrives. I expect that'll have to do. Bloody Knife, you might as well wait here too. Tell Varnum or the Colonel we'll scout on ahead. I expect you'll hear gunfire if we hit into them Lakota.

Curly swung aboard his dappled pony and, like the other Crow scouts, not all that anxious to continue on down the valley of the Rosebud. He cast a final look at the Arikara amidst the throes of their death chant, troubled, just a shade uneasy, but Curly knew it was an honor for one so young to be a scout. As he headed his horse to the south, he leaned down to snatch away from a thorny bush a couple of red roses, and as he rode he broke petals away to suck on them.

Hairy Moccasin smiled at this. "Signs of their presence are fresher, perhaps we'll come across them this morning."

Curly reached over and handed one of the roses to his Crow friend, and around a smile Curly said, "Those stones say they will have a great victory against the horse soldiers ... not against the Crow."

"Aiyyeee, perhaps. But what is to be, will be ..."

Photo courtesy of the Crow Nation.
Chief Plenty Coups was the principal Chief of the 135 Crow
warriors with Crook at the Rosebud. According to Crow oral
histories, if it were not for the leadership and warriors of Chief
Plenty Coups, General Crook and all of his bluecoat soldiers
would have been killed at the Battle of the Rosebud.

White Bull, a Minniconjou Sioux leader during the Battle of the Little Bighorn.
Photo courtesy of the Denver Public Library, Western History Collection,
Call Number: X-31427.

CHAPTER 3

Walks Alone:
e Rifle Presented to Him by His New Father

He was only twelve and slender as a willow. The rifle presented to him by his new father, Good Owl, was with Walks Alone wherever he went. Some of the other Miniconju boys were envious of his weapon. And, sensing that he had a wounded heart, some would taunt him so that his loneliness only deepened. Large luminous eyes reflected a grief which would not go away.

Two summers ago his mother had died in childbirth, the baby shortly thereafter. Only last winter his father had gone hunting and was killed by the Snakes. After that, he had been taken in by his father's brother, Good Owl.

The rifle was old. The stock had split after being dropped on some rocks, and he had repaired this by wrapping it with buffalo sinew. A few precious shells his new father had given him were carried at the waist in a doeskin pouch. Every day he would dart away from the lodge and take to the river banks, sometimes to fish, but mainly just to pretend he was firing the only possession he loved at some imaginary game, or the hated horse soldiers.

25

Before the Miniconju had left their winter valley to join the other Lakota tribes, he had been taken out by Good Owl and shown how to load and fire the old rifle. How good it felt snugged in against his cheek and shoulder! The kick, when he fired it, told Walks Alone of its killing powers.

Somehow he would always gravitate downriver to the northern part of the great encampment, to the area where Medicine Tail Creek cut down toward the eastern banks of the Greasy Grass. There he would always find some old men. They did not taunt him, as did some boys his own age. Some of the old men gave him their friendship and advice. He took in a trout cleaving the river surface dulled by the grayness of early morning, and it was gone in about the time it would take someone to blink. It served to remind Walks Alone that he had promised to go fishing at first light with one of the old grandfathers.

"I must not be late," he said, as he picked up his rifle and scrambled to his feet.

Across the river wooded scarps flowed by steep bluffs, above that the sky was bluing. Between the far bank and the beginnings of the bluffs stood a lonely ash in which reposed a nest of twigs and leaves made by a magpie.

A few other birds flitted over the river to dart into stands of larger trees where Walks Alone was passing.

It came to him that once he got a glimpse through the screening maze of lodges that his morning wandering had taken him far to the south. He was standing east of the Hunkpapa camp circle. Earlier he had heard riders bringing horses across the river, their distant shouts rising upon reaching the encampment.

Everyone was still talking about the great victory in the valley of the Rosebud. And it was possible that the one they defeated, Three Stars, was coming back to do battle again. If so, Walks Alone had his rifle. If the soldiers came, he would be with his friend, the old warrior, an old Oglala named Eagle That Talks. The talk in the encampment was that if the soldiers did come, the women, children, and old ones would flee west and north across the meadows and hide in the low hills.

If the soldiers did come, some of the old warriors and young boys would stay in the camps to help defend them.

As he dogtrotted around the trees and lashing bluestems and wheatgrass, from the taller cottonwoods fell feathery white cottony seeds. The feathery seeds caught in his hair. They clung to the shrubbery, and covered the ground. Passing into the clearing, he looked beyond the lodges and brush shelters toward the thousands of horses grazing and playing in bunches, duns, pintos, and bays, a profusion of colors and motion seen through the rising clouds of dust, the distant drumming of their hooves seeming to shake the ground.

Then, as he moved back into the trees, he became aware of another's presence. It was his friend, the Oglala warrior, near the water's edge. Walks Alone, in his eagerness, leaped over some low shrubbery only to have a foot become entangled. He fell.

When Walks Alone started to rise, he realized the Oglala was gazing at him in the most peculiar way. The boy dared not look away from the penetrating black eyes, wondering at the reason for such a look. Eagle That Talks came close and sat near the boy. Walks Alone sat back down. Both of them ignored the sounds of the awakening camps.

"We have had a late spring," said the Oglala as a sudden gust of wind plucked at his shirt fringes and whirled falling cottonwood seeds about in frenzied white patterns.

He went on, "The river is at its highest. Only then, my young friend, do the cottonwood trees let go of their seeds." He reached out a long-fingered and withered hand to touch Walks Alone's bare arm. "This was told to this old man by the spirits. In a dream last night they spoke of you ..."

The eyes of Eagle That Talks lidded over as he raised his

head slightly. And the boy, as he sat facing the old warrior, saw confusion dancing in the old eyes. He had not expected the honor of being in someone's dreams. He dared not speak, and Walks Alone could feel his heart beating faster.

"Sitting Bull," said the Oglala, upon looking up, "the great medicine-man of the Hunkpapa, spoke the truth about his vision."

He lifted a hand to let cottony seeds flutter into it.

"These seeds are a sign that something will happen in this valley … in this place we call Greasy Grass. Something strong. Something good, for our people."

He paused, the penetrating power of his eyes embracing those of Walks Alone, holding the boy in wondering silence.

"Yes, Grandson, something will happen here. And you will be part of it. This … my dream told me."

Looking down into the Medicine Tail Coulee,
looking into the site of the Indian encampment.
Photograph 2 of 10 sections of cylcorama by the Boston Cyclorama Co., 1889.
An 1889 representation of a portion of the huge Native-American
encampment at the Greasy Grass (the Little Bighorn).
Photo courtesy of the Library of Congress.

Currier & Ives: "Custer's Last Charge"
Photo Courtesy of the Library of Congress.

CHAPTER 4

Custer: Custer's Luck

Custer's luck.

This is what the Boy General's critics had called it during the Civil War. Custer's luck as the unwindings of Rosebud Creek revealed, for around every bend they came upon more abandoned camp sites.

Though a cloud shadow cut away the glare of the afternoon sun, it couldn't dim the luster of bony-white teeth bared in a pleased smile. The smile holding, the commander of the 7th Cavalry turned his sunburnt face to his adjutant riding alongside. "We have them now."

"Form the looks of it, General," replied lieutenant William Cooke, "the whole Sioux nation." He was a Canadian, a large man with a southerly wind tugging at his long side-whiskers.

At that moment George Armstrong Custer had a surge of affection for his adjutant. He could even forgive Major Reno's willful disregard of orders, in that Reno, while out on patrol, had crossed from the Tongue westward into the Rosebud valley. It was here Reno had come across Indian trails crossing to the south. And lost his chance for immortality, Custer had told him later in no uncertain terms, by not going after the hostiles. Out of this the ambitious Custer had sent out, through Mark Kellogg, a correspondent for both the *Bismarck Tribune* and Bennett's *New York Herald*, his slanted version of the Reno scouting expedition. But, Custer realized now, had Reno gone on the glory would have been his.

Achingly, he knew the upcoming fray would be the last big Indian fight on the Great Plains. The smile faded away. Into the deep-set eyes came a melancholic gleam. Since the Civil War it had been one battle heaped upon another. Glory after glory, for himself and the Regiment, his beloved 7th. A brilliant essayist, and a master of the phrase, he groped for words to describe his feelings from the many articles he'd written. He found these inadequate. Instead, there came this from General Sherman: "There is many a boy here today who looks upon war as all glory, but boys, it is all hell …"

But glory of a different kind Custer thought, awaited him, for the victor would become one of the Great Captains. Cadets at West Point would study his tactics, and it would be a springboard to the presidency. This was an ambition he shared with both Crook and Gibbon. But only he was hotly in pursuit of Indians numbering into the thousands, according to the Crow and Arikara scouts.

Hot after the mighty Sioux.

Custer's luck. Again the smile.

He had on a buckskin and a whitish, flat-crowned hat, the red scarf tied round his neck fluttering in the erratic breeze. Before his departure from Fort Abraham Lincoln, Libbie had shorn his locks. Somehow he still felt the touch of her hand, although the deeper he penetrated into the valley of the Rosebud his thoughts were not of her but that he had gotten rid of Terry keeping to the riverboat *Far West* until that worthy hooked-up with Gibbon.

How well he remembered the hot flush of shame when he had to get down on bended knee before General Alfred Terry. Out of it had come a telegram sent by Terry to President Grant begging that Lieutenant Colonel George Armstrong Custer be allowed to command the Seventh Cavalry again.

On bended knee, on bended knee, the moaning wind seemed to echo that refrain.

What brought all of this about were the charges he'd made against Secretary of War Belknap, the specifics that Belknap was profiteering in the revenues of traders at Army posts. This was bad enough, but he'd also accused President Grant's brother, Orville, of influence-peddling and receiving pay-offs. Under him the sorrel gelding, Vic, broke stride as if sensing Custer's anger. To have him bring a gloved hand rubbing along the gelding's mane, to say soothingly, "Easy does it, easy."

Behind Custer and Adjutant Cooke rode the standard-bearer, a corporal, holding a steadying hand against the staff of the swallow-tailed banner, Custer's personal emblem of red and blue with the crossed silver-white sabers, the wind rippling it overhead. Strung out two-by-two in a serpentine line passing out of sight around a bend in the creek was the Regiment. They'd be stretched out for a couple of miles, and to the concern of all officers, astride tired horses.

Until they reached the Yellowstone, some three-hundred and fifty miles due west out of Fort Abraham Lincoln, they'd maintained a gait which allowed the pack train to keep up.

Despite this, the horses had gaunted out. They needed more than the day's rest that had been allowed them. For the past two days, the harder pace coming down along the Rosebud had seen the pack train fall far behind. Some of the officers had voiced their concern to their commander. Glory won out, the glory that George Armstrong Custer knew was waiting for him in the heat of this summery month of June. Let me have them! My 7th can whip any fighting force in the world!

"So many roses, General."

Custer didn't respond as he gazed ahead down the narrow slot of valley. He had noticed the thick profusion of roses from which the valley derived its name, felt that a bouquet would be a nice present for Libbie. But where they rode, on the western side of the creek, and to both valley walls, the thorny stands of rose bushes had been crushed by what had passed through before.

Around those heading the column and roiled behind by the wind and by shod hooves rose a thick cloud of choking dust. Through the dust came deer flies to strike at horses. And there were buffalo gnats, swarming, tiny as circling dust particles, to bite at the eyelids until they swelled shut, to attack the ears so they swelled up. Battalion doctors had done what they could by having the men smear themselves with bear grease, or ashes, or spread their bandannas under their hats with a spot of coal oil to hold down the corners.

Now through the clearness ahead of the column, and even though the wind had picked up to send dust-devils spiraling back over the column, Custer and his adjutant took in the sudden appearance of Bloody Knife and three other Arikara scouts. But the scouts didn't come on but held out there, a good mile down the valley where it bent southwesterly.

"What do you make of it?" He'd said that more for his benefit than Cooke's.

Lieutenant Cooke, a quick glance to the sun sinking over the Little Wolfs, hawked spleen out of his mouth, then he said, "If there was trouble they'd be hightailing it in. Perhaps they've picked out a place to bivouac, sir."

"I expect that's it. I wonder how Bloody Knife is feeling ..." Custer uttered this in remembrance of how his favorite scout had slunk off with a bottle of whiskey last night.

Whiskey — another problem to cope with. Ever since they'd pulled out of the fort, whiskey peddlers had found them. And Reno, is he going to be a problem? Must have a chat with my second-in-command. Out here Custer had pushed away old animosities, grudges that seemed to build when soldiers were confined to an

Army post. But had Reno? Benteen? Others of their circle? Can't have that and survive. He knew from bitter experience that coming out victorious meant his delegating authority. That was simply it. There must be no indecision in time of crisis. But he had shown indecision the other night, of the 22nd. Mustn't let that happen again — not with what lay ahead, either here in the Rosebud or, as some of the officers had voiced, over in the Little Big Horn.

Spurring Vic into a canter, Cooke and his few staff officers and the guidon-bearer following, Custer had a smile for the benefit of the Arikaras. Coming on to them, the scouts wheeled in alongside, where Custer found himself riding next to Bloody Knife beginning to spout a message in broken English.

The gist of what Bloody Knife was saying was soon evident to the cavalrymen upon their coming over a short rise to take in the trampled valley floor spilling around the Sun Dance arbor and the sweat lodges.

Bloody Knife went on, "The Lakota are far to the south . . . how far we do not know . . . one day, maybe." He gestured with his hands. "But the Sun Dance is known to all the Plains Indians."

"How far south are my scouts?"

"A morning's ride away. Only the Crow and Lakota scouts went on."

Judging by the sun Custer knew it was sometime around five, knew he had every intention of pressing on until dusk. A short distance away the rest of the Arikara scouts squatted under gray-barked oaks, the sun at their backs. One he knew as Stabbed was chanting where he sat cross-legged by a smokeless fire with his head bobbing up and down. His death-song, mused Custer.

Reining up under a shading cottonwood, he told Cooke they would tarry here to rest and water the horses. Then Custer took in how the low, tawny hills forming the valley walls had given way to the ridges easterly, opposite the Little Wolfs humping up to around three-thousand feet, and on which firs were plentiful. And there were fewer thorny rose bushes. He took in Cooke carrying his orders to the column, while holding nearby on their horses were Bloody Knife and Lieutenant Varnum, who commanded the scouts.

Said Bloody Knife, "My people feel the Lakota have strong medicine." As did the other Ree scouts, he had on a long-sleeved shirt hanging loosely over worn trousers. His head was large with blunt features. Three eagle feathers were tucked in long shaggy hair, an Indian blanket was wrapped around his thick waist to hang down like a skirt above worn moccasins. For arms he carried a revolver, a Henry rifle, and a hunting knife.

He spoke again, "My people feel it was here Sitting Bull had a vision."

There was a short silence before Custer responded in a voice tinged with skepticism, "That so?"

"Over there in that sweat lodge we found painted rocks. They tell of many soldiers falling into camp."

"What do you make of it, Lo'tenant…"

Charles A. Varnum was possessed of a round head and small chin, and though in his middle twenties, a receding hairline. He had a deliberate manner, weighted everything he said, and as for Bloody Knife, he trusted the man's judgment, although he had reservations about the other Rees and the few Sioux scouting for them.

"As Bloody Knife said, Sitting Bull is their spiritual leader. We'll know more once the scouts return, I reckon around sundown."

"Yes, sundown," said Custer. "Seems they haven't sighted that Sioux camp, or they'd be back by now." He took another look at the Sun Dance arbor through pondering eyes.

"Sitting Bull, you say." Now to everyone there, "Well, we have stronger medicine."

"Sir, request permission for Bloody Knife and I to look for our scouts."

"Do so," replied Custer as he began walking his gelding toward the creek, to throw over his shoulder, "But you come across the Sioux, save some for us." Now he swung Vic sideways to watch Varnum and the Ree ride away.

Silently Custer murmured, "Terry's last words to me."

Now a gentle slap of his reins brought the gelding onto the creek bank.

* * * * * * *

Shadows were thickening in the valley when the Seventh Cavalry came in under a high bluff, where each company sought a place to camp. The pack train had managed to catch up, but the mules were left under pack, the horses chaffing under their saddles, some trying to roll on the dusty ground to rid themselves of the long day's sweat and dust and weariness. Ringing out were the frustrated cries of the recruits, the curses of sergeants or officers, as they attempted to keep the horses from scattering out too quickly to patches of lush grass. Because down here at the lower end of the Rosebud Valley the Sioux hadn't made camp but had kept on the move.

Under the prow of the bluff there was no wind, and the air was stifling and clammy hot, the valley thick with oak and willow, with brush and more trees cutting up into draws further to the south. Small campfires began glowing to cut the gloom of this dying day.

Came a whisper passing through the bivouac that the Arikara scouts had been sent northwesterly in search of Gibbon and Terry. Old campaigners predicted they'd be on the move again before midnight. Of more importance to the recruits were their aches and pains and private fears.

Custer's "Dog Robber," ancient and white-bearded Private John Burkman, had put up the Colonel's tent. A fire crackling and a folding chair out front, Burkman had set about heating some rations. Officially he was assigned to Lieutenant Calhoun's L Company. He'd taken notice of Custer issuing orders to Stabbed and some other Arikaras, left what he saw back there among the trees. Around the tent and up to the fire came Custer, and from where Burkman hunkered their eyes locked.

"How old are you, John?"

"Not old enough to be your great grandpappy" — a belated afterthought — "sir." Deep furrows passed between rheumy blue eyes, with suspenders holding up baggy trousers tucked into scuffed boots. "Coffee's perking."

Slumping onto the chair, Custer reached up a weary hand and removed his hat, his hand sagging down alongside the chair to dislodge dust from his coat. As Burkman held out a tin cup, Custer peeled off his gauntleted gloves before crooking a finger through the handle of the cup, then he said gently, "John, commencing at sun-up I'm assigning you to the pack train."

Testily Burkman said, "Didn't sign on to be no doggone muleskinner." But he let it go at that, the expression on Custer's face that of a man torn by deep emotions, burdened down with command. A final question: "We'll be pulling out at eleven tonight?"

A nod from Custer brought the orderly back to the business at hand. As for the commander of the 7th Cavalry, he let the sounds, smells, the sight of faces long familiar to him be the balm he needed to shred his fears of what tomorrow would bring. Seemed cavalry blue was all he'd known for too many years, knew he had served his country well. But when one attained higher rank, well, one attained other enemies than the Rebs of the Civil War, or Plains Indians. He reached for the tin plate held out by Burkman, ate what it contained, soaked it down with more coffee, as drifting over to his fire came Mark Kellogg.

The little news hawk said cheerily, "Seems everything's going your way, General ..." Thick black brows hung above a long nose, and he was clean-shaven, with long black sideburns. Duffing his straw hat, purchased from any Army sutler, he sank down to Custer's right, eagerly waiting for a response from his hero.

"We shall have after them, pursue them," Custer said soberly. "Have you had further words with Reno?" En route to their rendezvous along the Yellowstone, there'd been an encounter of words between the major and Kellogg over Kellogg's presence with the 7th. Reno had called the reporter Custer's tout, even though Kellogg was here with the full sanction of General Terry.

"I have studiously avoided that worthy."

"Better that way." He trusted Kellogg. Had to trust the news hawk, for Kellogg's dispatches were his only means of communicating with eastern newspapers. Once he was in the White House there'd be a job for the young reporter.

Looming above another officer, the pair of them having just come across the creek, was Adjutant Cooke, and as usual, carrying on an animated conversation, the ends of those magnificent muttonchops bouncing against his dark blue blouse. Both officers settled in around a fire being stoked with more wood by Custer's orderly. Then Burkman left to lay down his saddle blanket and catch what sleep he could.

Others drifted over, the circle spreading around the campfire, with Custer letting the talk swirl around him, as his thoughts were elsewhere. The scouts … should have returned by now. Haven't heard gunfire. It was a lot darker now, or perhaps it was just this bluff cutting away the western horizon.

Not all that distant he took in another campfire, Benteen's. Gathered there were the Irishmen, Captain Keogh, and his Lieutenant, Porter, a handful more, held spellbound by yarns told by Lieutenant De Rudio in his thick Italian-English. While Benteen had tucked in under his saddle blanket to lay with his hands cupped behind his head, listening. The notion was there to break away and go over, wish his officers well over what tomorrow would bring. But Benteen's presence held him to the chair. And of Reno there was no sign. Nor did he expect there would be.

The talk at Custer's fire broke away with the appearance of

a sergeant, who slipped to Custer's side. At the word the scouts were back, Custer rose briskly, but left his hat and gloves by the chair. Out of the night came Varnum, guides Bouyer, Reynolds, and the Negro Dorman, lastly Half Yellow Face, leader of the Crow scouts. Now the early moon had slipped away. Around them in the near-darkness came the restless neigh and stamping of horses, quiet chatter, voices raised in song beyond some brush. He let Varnum take over, Custer a trifle anxious, and everyone left the fire to come in closer.

Tersely Lieutenant Varnum said, "No question but that they'll be headed into the Little Big Horn. And, sir, we're not all that far behind. The scouts spoke of a high hill, maybe about twenty miles down the valley, a place on it called the Crow's Nest nestled up on the divide."

"Speaking of something doesn't make it fact," retorted Custer. "I've got to know. What about the Sioux, did you see any?"

Lonesome Charlie Reynolds cleared his throat as he pushed closer. A Kentuckian, he was quiet to the point of being shy, but he knew better'n any white man these Plains Indians. It was Reynolds who had carried the first message describing the discovery of gold in the Black Hills westward to Fort Laramie, a ride of over a hundred miles through Sioux-infested territory. An infection to his trigger hand had left it swollen, the bandage around his hand grimed with dust.

He said, "We found a fresher trail coming in from the east. A bunch of around a hundred and fifty. It's possible they could have spotted us. Headed into the Little Big Horn same's the main party of Sioux."

"This only confirms," Custer said worriedly, "my decision to move out at eleven. Sorry, Varnum, but you and your scouts will have to head for this lookout point, the Crow's Nest. Grab what you can to eat. Saddle fresh horses. Then move out. The rest of you, I suggest you get what sleep you can."

As the scouts and his officer dispersed, Lieutenant Colonel George A. Custer fought down a mingling of anxiety and excitement. If his scouts had been spotted, the Sioux might break camp and strike for the Big Horns. Which meant his decision to make a night march was correct. He turned at the scuffling of boots, let a delighted smile turn his concerns away. There, to have a delightful nightcap of words with him, were his brothers Tom and Boston, and their nephew, Autie Reed.

"Should have some coffee left," he said graciously. A laugh for the way Autie Reed lowered cautiously to sit down on the ground; smiles from the others. "So, this has proved out to be more than a picnic."

Boston Custer said, "We've been sorely pushed, for sure, Colonel. But, it's worth it being here."

"Where's our brother-in-law ..." Custer was speaking of Lieutenant James Calhoun. He was married to Margaret Custer, and like the Custers hailed from Monroe, Michigan.

In response Tom Custer said, "Asleep with the rest of his company." He waved his hand. "No, no coffee. George, we've got to talk . . ."

Reclaiming the chair, Custer nodded.

"Mind you, I'm not speaking for the other company commanders. Just that, our horses are tuckered out. Even if those Indians broke away, be awful hard to catch them."

"Tom, I can't risk waiting until morning. Not at all. This is our golden opportunity" — he smashed a clenched fist down at his knee — "to get the victory. Crook, Gibbon, they want the same thing."

"Victory; I pray so." Tom Custer, a holder of two Congressional Medals of Honor, and five years younger than his more famous brother, acquiesced with a tired smile. More than Boston or Autie Reed, he knew the pressures his brother was under. From the President, the Department of the Army, from with

41

in his own beloved 7th. His face brightening, he reached out and gripped Custer's forearm.

"We've always stood together. With luck, a victory tomorrow will see your dream realized."

"Custer's luck?"

"Custer's luck, it's never let us down before."

Custer's Buckskin Coat
Photo by: Rich Strauss
Courtesy of: the Smithsonian Institution

The encampment along theLittle Big Horn.
Photograph 3 of 10 sections of cylcorama
by the Boston Cyclorama Co., 1889.
Reproduction number: LC-USZ61-22 through USZ61-31
Photo courtesy of the Library of Congress.

"Beyond the Little Bighorn,"
1908 photo by Richard Throssell.
Courtesy of the Denver Public Library.
Call Number: X-31207.

CHAPTER 5

The Camp

Seven days had passed since the fight with Three Stars at Rosebud Creek. Scouts had returned from the south to report that Three Stars and his army had moved away past Goose Creek, two days' ride from the Greasy Grass. Many in the sprawling camp hoped that Three Stars' going would mean that the bluecoats would stay away. Perhaps the sting of shame over the defeat on Rosebud Creek would cause the soldiers to think before attacking the Lakota, the way they had attacked He Dog's camp on the Little Powder River.

On the other hand, perhaps they would be hot for revenge. But Three Stars was not acting like a soldier leader with revenge on his mind. He was behaving more like a dog who had been caught trying to steal from the meat racks, skulking away with his tail tucked under in submission.

The talk inside the lodges and around the outside fires was that Three Stars was no longer to be feared. But what about reports from the north, from the Yellowstone Country, some asked.

45

Soldiers were up in that area, too. Three Stars was one thing, but soldiers in the north country was another, some said. That was the worry. There were many, many whites. Whites who were soldiers were fewer than whites who were putting up houses and tearing up the land to plant their crops. Then there were the uncountable numbers who had traveled westward along the Holy Road south of the Shell River several winters ago. Then the gold seekers, who had made a path through the best hunting country of the Lakota, had been a problem. They had laid out a road going north, just east of the Shining Mountains and on into Crow and Blackfeet country. Because of that road, three soldier forts had been built in the middle of Lakota hunting grounds. And eight winters past, the Oglala Lakota led by Red Cloud had forced the bluecoats to abandon the one on Little Piney Creek. That fort had been set on fire almost before the last soldier had gone.

The whites were much trouble because they were many, and because they wanted the land. And those in camp who thought that dwelling on Three Stars would be foolish quietly reminded others about all of these happenings. "Crazy Horse is right," an old, old man said to a warrior grandson. "It is time to put an end to the white man in our lands."

Yesterday the people had moved their lodges north from Ash Creek. It had not been a long move, but it had been a happening to behold. Never in recent memory had so many people gathered here. This area near the Greasy Grass Creek was a favorite place for such summer gatherings. But the gathering this summer was different. Different because of the ever-growing problem of the whites. And different because of the number of people.

Camp criers, old men strong of voice and reputation, moved through camp circles after sun-up announcing the move north to Greasy Grass Meadow. At first only a few lodges came down here and there. But before too long, lodges were coming down with nearly every heartbeat. Travoises and pack horses were laden with lodges, now rolled into tight bundles, and other household things. Painted rawhide parfleches. Clothing bags. Rolled-up backrests. Sleeping and sitting robes.

Women gathered small children to them. Babies in cradle boards were slung over the back or hung on the front fork of saddles. Before the sun was halfway to its mid-day point, no lodges were standing. An old man firecarrier had gathered embers from the fire in the council lodge to carry to the new camp. A symbol of the continuity of life. He joined an old medicine-man at the northern edge of the mass of waiting people. Together they rode at the front as the short trek began.

Like a wolf waking from a nap, the great mass slowly stretched, lengthening from north to south until there was one long moving body providing sights and sounds to stir the heart. The ground shook and a noise like thunder filled the air as the horse herds were moved. Thousands of drag poles from the travoises raised dust to hang like a cloud caught near the ground. Young boys raced their horses at the edges of the great moving mass of people and animals. Dogs barked and children shouted. People were awestruck into silence at being part of such a great thing. Some warriors, sitting on their along high bluffs just east across the river from the new camp, watched in reverence as the wide stream of humanity moved northward.

The move was done with the same quiet purpose of a wolf mother moving her pups from one den to another. Lakota women could take down a lodge in as much time as it took for the sun to move across the floor of one. They could pitch it just as quickly. No one shouted orders, yet the old camp was taken down and the new one put in order because everyone knew what had to be done. And it was done.

It had begun after sun-up, and before the sun was near the edge of the western horizon the new camp was in place. By the time the sun went down and evening cooking fires flickered like stars, the enormous dust cloud was finally thinning out. People settled in. The sprawling camp was if it had always been there.

This particular place was a favorite because of the groves of cottonwood trees near the river and west of it into the meadow. And there was enough grass in the broad floor of the valley to feed thousands of horses for many days. The lodges were pitched among the cottonwoods in several large circles, cleverly hidden from the probing eyes of enemy scouts.

The horse herds were to the west and north. Most of the horse watchers were boys, but around the herds were warriors standing guard. East across the river, atop some of the sharply rolling hills and a few bluffs to the south, small groups of warriors were likewise on guard. But it was generally felt that no enemy would be foolish enough to come close to such a large and powerful encampment. From within, it was a thing to behold. The countless lodges stretched a great distance along the Greasy Grass, far, far beyond the cast of even the strongest sinew-backed bow. Some of the people walked to the high bluffs across the river to look back toward Ash Creek, just to see the wide swath left on earth by the travois drag poles.

The trail left by the drag poles was wide and deep. A sign left by a people who lived on the Earth and with it. It was well known that the drag poles loosened the earth and allowed new grass to grow faster. In time the darkness of the wide trail would turn to green.

On the seventh evening after the fight with Three Stars an old, old warrior walked slowly through the camp. After a time he would grow tired, then rest and walk again. Tears flowed down his face as he walked, tears of joy and sadness. He was joyful for such a gathering, because he had not seen such a sight for many, many winters. He was sad because he knew it would be the last to happen in his lifetime.

Uses Cane was nearly eighty winters old. Born in a time when the whites in Lakota country were like an occasional drop from a slowly melting icicle, he had watched their coming grow into a menacing flood. That was another reason for his sadness, and he prayed that this great gathering would not be the last for many lifetimes to come.

But the whites had brought much with them. Much that was not good for the Lakota, and other peoples of the Earth.

Change was the main thing. Life for the Lakota had changed rapidly with the coming of the whites. While still a warrior in his prime, Uses Cane had seen the smallpox sickness sweep through the Lakota living near the Great Muddy River. And later, news came from the north that the People-who-lived-in-earth-lodges had been all but wiped out by that dreadful sickness. A white man sickness, brought up from the south country by one of the fire boats that traveled on the Great Muddy River.

Uses Cane was a Sicangu, one of the Burnt Thigh People. Dark liquid eyes beneath the furrowed old brows missed very little, even though they had dimmed with his great age. Snow-white hair, having long ago lost the black luster of youth, hung nearly to his waist. His head was unadorned and he walked with a cane. Long ago, while still a stalwart warrior, he had driven his stake rope into the ground in a fight with a Pawnee near the Niobrara River. He did not retreat, but he did suffer a grievous wound because the Pawnee had guns. A ball through the right hip had thrown him to the earth. But his courage lifted his fellow Sicangu warriors past their fears and the Pawnee were defeated. Not one of them lived to carry the news of their shameful defeat back to the south country.

The old warrior had started his walk in his own camp circle and moved slowly south, past the Itazipacola and Miniconju camps. A cooking fire was burning at nearly every lodge. Women, young and old, prepared meals for their families. Some lodges had visitors waiting patiently and politely to be fed. Children were everywhere, flitting about like flocks of small, quick birds. Or careening between lodges like herds of bouncing antelope.

Many lodges had a tripod of sapling standing to the right of the east-facing door. On the tripods were the things of a hunter and warrior. A long buffalo hunting lance and a shorter war lance. A war club. A bow in its finely quilled or beaded case, attached to a quiver filled with arrows. The shield was arranged at the center. And sometimes there was a rifle inside a long, decorated hide case. Above, amidst the streamers tied to the tall, slender lodgepoles, were a few scalp locks, an indication of the prowess and reputation of the warrior who lived in the lodge.

Here and there sat small groups of old ones. They talked about the days far in the past, of people no longer on this journey, of this hunt or that war party. They spoke of their grandchildren, and asked after relatives. And they tried to decide when last the people had gathered together in such numbers as in this encampment.

Warriors stood in small circles or sat around a fire. They compared weapons, relived the Rosebud fight, traded horses, and talked about the good elk hunting in the Shining Mountains.

Most men, young and old, were dressed in leggings, breechcloth, and moccasins. Older men wore an elk or deerhide hairshirt. Some of the younger men wore a breastplate. And some of those who had lately come from a reservation were dressed in white man's clothes. A few wore leggings made from blue tradecloth. Women and girls wore tanned hide dresses made from elk or deer hide, moccasins and calf-length leggings. Most wore quilled, beaded, or silver concho belts, from which hung a knife just at the small of the back. Here and there was someone in a dress of blue calico.

Most of the warriors and old men wore at least one eagle feather tied into the hair. Some wore elaborate fans with as many as eight feathers in a bunch. A feather was more than adornment or simple decoration. Each was earned, on the hunt or in battle.

Uses Cane saw all of these good things, and felt the power of this great encampment.

Inside the Hunkpapa camp, a young woman came to him

and conveyed an invitation to come and eat inside one of the lodges. The old warrior spoke his thanks and followed her. Inside a comfortable Hunkpapa lodge he was given the place of honor at the back, opposite the door. He did not know this family. Soon, the young woman came in with a bowl of elk rib stew. Uses Cane took the food, offering heartfelt appreciation. When he had finished eating, he went out of the lodge and held out the empty bowl to the girl.

"Here is your dish, Granddaughter," he said. "It was the best elk rib stew this old man has ever eaten."

With a smile the girl took back the bowl. As he walked away, the old man lifted his voice in an honor song for this Hunkpapa lodge. Such was the way of the Lakota. He did not know them by name. They did not know him. But he was an old warrior, and this particular Hunkpapa family had lost a revered grandfather two winters past. In his honor, they fed every old man who came near their lodge.

Day was waning. Night was coming strong from the east. The old warrior sat for a rest beneath an ancient cottonwood. Growing darkness sharpened the light from the cooking fires.

From the Hunkpapa camp the old warrior bent his feeble steps to the north, until he found himself among the Oglala. Picketed near the door of a lodge was a tan and white mare, Crazy Horse's favorite mount. Suddenly, the great warrior emerged from the lodge, untied the mare, swung onto her back, and rode away into the maze of people, lodges, and cottonwoods. For a brief moment, the old warrior bemoaned his frail body and yearned for the strength of his prime. He would gladly give up all the days left on his life's journey to follow that great warrior just once.

After a time, the bright spots of firelight among the lodges and cottonwoods seemed like a patch of the night sky with its shimmering stars. Like the stars, the fires seemed to dance as their flames bent to the whims of soft breezes. Then, from somewhere in the depths of the camp, a drum began a muffled beat, a beat steady and persistent, in time with hundreds of fires in the great encampment along the Greasy Grass. The old warrior shuffled through a few steps of a scalp dance, and muttered a prayer.

"Grandfather," he cried, "you have let a pitiful old man see this great thing. I am thankful."

The encampment along theLittle Big Horn.
Photograph 9 of 10 sections of cylcorama by the Boston Cyclorama Co., 1889.
Reproduction number: LC-USZ61-22 through USZ61-31
Photo courtesy of the Library of Congress.

Red Cloud
Courtesy of the Denver Public Library, Western History Collection,
photo by D. F. Barry (1886),
Call Number: B-115

Sitting Bull,
Photograph by Palmquist and Jurgens, 1884.
Courtesy of the Smithsonian Institution.

Sitting Bull

To the east, across the river, the sounds of the great encampment reached the ears of a solitary figure standing on the pinnacle of a hill. He was Hunkpapa. A holy man. He was Sitting Bull.

He had passed the evening immersed in prayer. "Have pity on the people," he had prayed. "Look with kindness on the young and the old ones, all the helpless ones. Look most with pity on those who must lead, those who must show us the way to find good answers for the difficult things which lay in our road. Give them clear minds to think well. Give them strong hearts to do what must be done ..." He had left a ring of willow sticks in the dry earth. Tied to each was a small bundle of tobacco. An offering.

He sat now just below the crest of a hill, a stone's throw from the circle of tobacco ties. Across the river and below he could see the countless fires casting a red glow against lodges and trees. This gathering was strong. Three Stars had learned that, now somewhere to the south, licking his wounds and moving his soldiers away.

Some months back, Sitting Bull had sent word to all parts of the nation. "Say that the Lakota should gather in the summer," he told his messengers. And there was a need for that. Many things, difficult to understand, had happened over the past few winters. The reason for all of those puzzling things was the white man. Sitting Bull had perceived a feeling among the people, like the one weak strand in a bowstring. Many of the people began to think that the white man could never be driven away. For that reason, he had called for a gathering. A renewal was needed. The people needed to remember that their strength grew when they thought alike and moved down the same road together. Now, as he looked at the size of the encampment, as he tried to count the glowing fires, he was certain that things were happening as they had been meant to happen. It was good.

Still, there was something that did not fit. The answer for which was difficult to see.

It had to do with the vision coming from the Sun Dance. Amidst the pain, out of the swirl of sound and color, from the domain beyond this Earth, had come the picture of bluecoat soldiers falling head-first into the circle of a Lakota camp. A picture with images so real he could smell the odor of warm blood. The blood of soldiers. The blood of horse soldiers. And when he spoke of this vision, a new certainty flowed through the people like a prairie fire driven by a relentless wind. Warriors had carried that certainty with them to the valley of the Rosebud, seven days ago. That certainty helped them to defeat Three Stars and his army.

Still, that victory had not been the victory foretold in the vision. Sitting Bull was certain of that. Was there another victory yet to come? Yes. He was certain of that, too. And that meant that Three Stars might turn his army around to find the warriors who had beaten him, to wipe the bile of defeat from his mouth. But, a few scouts had returned from the Yellowstone River country with news of soldiers there.

There was one thing that was certain. Soldiers were coming.

The vision was not an empty and meaningless thing. And it would come to pass. Yet he did not know why soldiers would attack such a strong camp. But the why of it was no longer important. That soldiers would come was the important thing. They would attack a Lakota camp. Perhaps this one. Perhaps another. It was their way. They had attacked many Lakota camps. They had killed women and children. It was their way. And friends of the Lakota, the Cheyenne, still spoke of Sand Creek and the Washita River with grief in the heart and bitterness in the voice.

There was much that needed to be avenged. Perhaps many soldiers falling into a Lakota camp would be part of that. But there must be an ending, Sitting Bull thought. Crazy Horse's words in the council before the Rosebud Fight were true. There must be an end to the white man in Lakota country.

The medicine-man gazed at the hundreds of fires in the encampment. If ever there was a time for the Lakota, their relatives, and their allies to gather their power and move as one against the whites, it was now. Many people were here now, from all parts of the nation. Oglala, Sihasapa, Itazipacola, Miniconju, Hunkpapa, Sicangu, and Isanti. The Sahiyela had many lodges here, too.

Many important and powerful men were here now. Red On top of the Isanti, Gall, Crow King, and Black Moon of Sitting Bull's Hunkpapa. He Dog of the Sicangu. Two Moons of the Sahiyela. Touch the Clouds and Elk Head — Keeper of the Sacred Pipe — of the Itazipacola. Big Road and Crazy Horse of the Oglala.

Any enemy would be foolish to stand in the path of such power. Only the white man would. He who spoke empty promises and killed women and children. Old enemies, like the Pawnee, Snakes, Crow, and Blackfeet, were people of the Earth. To fight them was to fight enemies who knew the Earth, and the meaning of honor. Not so the whites. The whites, as a group, were no speakers of truth. They were bringers of death for the peoples of the Earth. They raised one hand in peace while the other held a gun. So now must be the time. The Hunkpapa medicine-man knew there would be no time better. The people must remember that their way was the circle. All parts of it must be strong for it to remain whole. Weakness would break the circle, and that would mean victory for the white man.

Sitting Bull knew that these thoughts must be spoken in the council lodge. Tomorrow he would ask for a gathering of the old men leaders and the younger ones with strong following. They must be convinced that to think alike regarding the white man was the best way. There was a time to ignore the mosquito, but there was also a time to swat … before he took blood, not after. The white man had taken much. It was past the time for swatting.

Tomorrow, he would ask for a council. He would choose his words carefully. To touch the hearts of those who show the way, he must first turn their minds. Tomorrow could foretell if a gathering such as this would happen again. Yes. Tomorrow he must choose his words carefully.

Sitting Bull gathered his things and stood. From within the encampment came the ring of many drums. There was a soft splashing in the water somewhere below him. Within the folds of darkness floated the clear notes of a flute. A courting song. He smiled. Life. As it should be. He stared down the steep slope toward the river, moccasins swishing the sparse grass. At the river he removed them and stepped into the cool water, crossing slowly to let the water soothe his feet. On the west bank he passed a young warrior watering two horses. Nearby was a brush shelter so well hidden in the willows that he nearly walked into it. Two young men sat at a low fire. One was making war arrows and the other rubbed an old rifle with a soft piece of buckskin. The arrow maker looked up, and stood when he recognized the man in his firelight.

Sitting Bull was a striking figure. He wore a smoked deer-hide shirt. Two wide strips of green-dyed porcupine quillwork ran from near the points of his shoulders to the waistline. The bottom edges of the shirt were fringed, as were the upper portions of the sleeve down to the elbows. Among the sleeve fringes, and hanging from the shoulders, were long, thin locks of human hair. Leggings and moccasins were decorated with the same pattern as the quill strips on the shirt. The breechcloth was red. Beneath the shirt he wore a quilled belt, and from it hung a knife in its decorated sheath. The knife was the only weapon he carried this night.

The second young man came to his feet, as both young men smiled and nodded shyly. "Grandfather," the arrow maker said, "it is good to see you."

The medicine-man paused. "I am glad to see you here," he told them. "And it is good to see a young man doing something in the old way," he observed, looking at the arrow in the first young man's hand. And quickly, to chase away a sudden look of dismay in the eyes of the young man with the rifle, he said, "And sometimes new things are good. The white man is a doubtful thing, but his guns are good … in Lakota hands."

Both young men smiled and uttered an affirmation. "You are comfortable here?" Sitting Bull wanted to know. The young men nodded emphatically. "Good," the medicine-man said. "And where did you come from?"

"From near the Smoking Earth River," replied the arrow maker.

"You are Sicangu?"

They nodded again. The arrow maker said, "I am called White Feather Tail. My cousin here is Bear. We arrived four days ago."

Sitting Bull nodded. "It makes my heart glad to see you here."

White Feather Tail, tall and muscular, held out the arrow he had just finished. "It is not a very good arrow," he said. "But it will fly straight. And it is something for you to remember us by."

Sitting Bull took the arrow and appraised it with glowing eyes. The young man was wrong. It was a fine arrow. It was made by one with much skill in the hands and knowing in the heart.

"This is a fine thing," he told the arrow maker. "I am thankful. I will mark it with red. And now, you must both come to my lodge. I am hungry and would like for you to eat with me."

There was much activity around the lodge of the Hunkpapa medicine-man. Inside, a very low fire sent out a soft glow. A woman playing with a small boy looked up as Sitting Bull entered with his two guests. "These young men are hungry. And I have told them that your cooking is the best in this camp," he told her, a soft smile playing on his wide mouth. She returned his smile and nodded. Soon, she had food for everyone. In the middle of the meal there came a soft scratching at the door. It was a boy with a message from one of the medicine-man's relatives. A beloved old woman, an aunt, was ill unto dying. His help was needed.

Sitting Bull gathered his pipe bag and other medicine things. Before he ducked out the door, he paused and looked back at the two young Sicangu warriors. "Make certain your bowstrings are taut," he cautioned. "Count your arrows and your bullets. It is good to be ready."

Captain Tom Custer, of C Company, 7th Cavalry. Tom Custer was so brave that, for actions performed during the American Civil War, he was twice awarded the Congressional Medal of Honor. (Both Medals of Honor are visible in this picture.)
Courtesy of the Denver Public Library, Western History Collection,
photo by D. F. Barry (1879),
Call Number: B-53

Chief Gall of the Dakota.
Courtesy of the Denver Public Library, Western History
Collection, photograph taken by D. F. Barry,
probably in or about 1881,
Call Number: B-84.

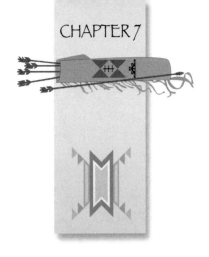

CHAPTER 7

A Warning

A cool breeze danced along the dark slopes of the hills to the east of the camp. It carried a soft sound to the ears of two warrior sentinels sitting near a clump of soapweed. A soft sound that did not fit into the myriad of usual night noises. Red Hair, so called because of the streaks of reddish highlights in his hair, touched his companion on the arm. Good Hand nodded, indicating that he, too, had heard the out-of-place sound. They were both Hunkpapa, companions since boyhood. Now, just past their teens, they already shared many hunts and more than a few warriors' trails. Good Hand quickly strung his bow, which had been encased in his lap. Red Hand fingered his war lance and strained his ears for the sound. It came again, closer this time.

Footsteps, soft but distinguishable. They were not those of deer or elk. The four-leggeds had moved away from the large encampment, beyond the reach of arrow and bullet. The noise was not made by the furtive movements of a nervous rabbit. The footsteps were those of a two-legged. Plainly with reason to move cautiously toward camp.

The two young warriors flattened, belly-down, bending in with the sparse blades of grass on the dry earth, eyes on the skyline. Hearts pounded a little faster and a dryness like dust caught in their mouths as the footsteps came even closer, just beyond the crest of the rise. A vague upright shape appeared, darker than the surrounding night sky, less than a stone toss from the still motionless warriors. The shape slowly shrank as if sliding down into the earth. It did not move for a time. When both young warriors were certain that the dark shape could hear their pounding hearts, it rose up again. And came closer.

Red Hair saw the outline of the man's head. He had stopped again, not more than two body lengths from the hidden Lakota. The Hunkpapa thought the outline of the head resembled the hairstyle of a Crow warrior. Then, as the man leaned slightly forward, Red Hair glimpsed the strands of a Crow-style necklace. The young Lakota warrior pinpointed the other night sounds, one by one, searching for the sounds of other footsteps. There were none. This Crow, this foolish Crow, was alone. The man rose and stole down the slope, passing between the two prone Lakota. Red Hair thrust his lance quickly between the moving ankles of the Crow, sending the man face-down into the dusty slope. In two heartbeats the Lakota warriors had the intruder pinned heavily to the earth.

"Friend! Friend!" The muffled words, clearly Lakota, came from the face shoved into the dirt. They came in time to stop the downward thrust of Red Hair's lance toward the intruder's neck.

The two Hunkpapa warriors looked at one another. It was not the first time either of them had heard a Crow speak Lakota words. Plainly, this man was a scout. Perhaps picked to sneak close to the Lakota encampment because he could understand the language. "Friend! Friend!" the intruder repeater. "I come without weapons."

Good Hand pulled the man over onto his back and placed the blade of his knife against the quivering throat. "Then you are stupid," he said. "That only makes it easier to kill you!"

The captive's eyes shifted fearfully. "No! No! I do not want you to kill me!"

Good Hand pushed the knife blade harder against the throat. "Then why do you come here, sneaking up on our camp?"

"I have something to tell the great one, Sitting Bull."

The two Hunkpapa exchanged a puzzled look. Red Hair leaned closer and studied the man. He was a Crow. His hair was not as long as some Crows wore theirs, but it was slicked back on top. The face was wide, with a long, square jaw. Eyes were set apart wide above the straight, prominent nose. He wore Crow leggings, moccasins, and breechcloth. Beneath the strands of the necklace was a soldier's blue coat with the sleeves cut off.

"The leader of the Hunkpapa Lakota has no need of your words," Red Hair told the Crow. "He is not interested in what a sneaking Crow would have to say."

The captive continued to shift his nervous gaze between the two young Lakota. "I have word about the bluecoat soldiers."

"We know about the bluecoats," hissed Good Hand, maintaining the pressure with his knife. "We spanked them at Rosebud Creek. Now they are going back south licking their wounds."

The Crow's eyes widened a little. "There are others," he said. "A day's ride from here. East, beyond the Wolf Mountains. Higher up the Rosebud."

Good Hand gazed long at the frightened face. "We know that the Crow and Snakes scout for the bluecoats. I think the bluecoats sent you here."

"It is true. My people, some of them, scout for the soldiers. The bluecoats did not send me. I do not scout for them!"

Red Hair leaned closer. "Then how is it you know about them? How is it that you know where they are?"

The captive licked his dry lips. "I watch them. For many days I have been following them."

"Why?" Red Hair wanted to know.

The man shrugged. "I do not like them. I wish for the Lakota to kill them all."

Red Hair looked at his companion. He could not believe this Crow, this enemy quivering under Good Hand's knife. But he was certain of one thing. Sitting Bull and the other leaders in the camp must be told of this intruder. They would decide what to do about this Lakota-speaking Crow. Red Hair motioned to his companion. Together they pulled the man to his feet. "We will take him to our uncle," he said to Good Hand. "He will …"

A sudden, powerful shove sent each warrior sprawling to the dirt. They were both up in an instant, but it was too late. The Crow had disappeared into the darkness, though they could hear the sound of running feet. Good Hand bolted forward but Red Hair grabbed his arm. "No!" he warned. "There could be others waiting in the dark. More than we could handle."

Although angry, Good Hand saw the wisdom in his brother friend's words. "Still, our uncle must know about this!"

Red Hair agreed.

At the lodge of Sitting Bull, they were told that he was at the home of Four Horns, tending to an old woman. They hurried to the lodge of Four Horns. There, a man, a helper to the Hunkpapa medicineman this night, quietly told the anxious warriors that Sitting Bull must not be interrupted. "You can wait," the man told them.

The young Hunkpapa warriors pushed their request only a little more before they yielded to the helper's quiet insistence. They retreated to a fallen log near Four Horn's lodge, talking in low tones to one another. It was nearly dawn. A faint glow rimmed the eastern horizon. Birds roosting in the cottonwoods began to announce the new day. Far off across the river to the east, where the two young warriors had taken down the Crow, a meadow lark sang its bright song.

Even as the camp began to stir with the coming of the new day, a keening arose from within the lodge of Four Horns. Death had come there with the new day. Sitting Bull emerged shortly, his dark face downcast. He glanced around and recognized the two young warriors on the log. They stood and he approached them.

"Uncle, there is something we must tell you."

The Hunkpapa medicine-man listened implacably to the story told by the two young men. When they finished, he said, "Say nothing of this to anyone. I am going to ask for a council, and I will speak to the leaders of this thing you tell me."

A young man sitting behind a tree waited until he was sure the three Hunkpapa were well on their way before he stood. He had heard the quiet conversation about the Crow intruder. He was certain that the great Oglala war leader would want to know what he just heard.

"Home of the River Crows"
View of Crow tepees along the banks of the Little Bighorn (Greasy Grass) River in the Blacklodge district of the Crow Reservation, Montana.
Photo courtesy of the Denver Public Library, Western History Collection, photograph by Richard Throssel, 1911,
Call Number: X-31211.

George Armstrong Custer, as a Major-General.
Photo from the period of the War Between the States.
Photo courtesy of The Library of Congress.

CHAPTER 8

Custer: Into the Valley of Death

Sunday - June 25, 1876

Into the Valley of Death . . . . .

He had not slept, simply could not let go of what was to come. The burden of command: his alone. He mused: What were the plans of Crook coming up from the south? To attack, most assuredly, and gain the glorious victory.

"But I've got the edge," the commander of the 7th Cavalry gloated inwardly. He knew they were at least twenty-four hours ahead of schedule.

They would have the glory.

There was still some worry, for despite the fact the Regiment had headed out an hour ago, leaving behind Thompson's Creek where it adjoined with the Rosebud, the going had been arduously slow. Out front with Custer were Girard, a former trader and the interpreter for the Ree, and Half Yellow Face, leader of the Crow scouts. Although they were supposed to be out front picking the trail, their shared worries kept them hanging in alongside Yellow Hair.

The Regiment was spread out company-by-company. The stars were bright above but were obscured by dust rising in blinding clouds. Southwesterly lightning flickered low along the horizon, but too far away to even outline the bony ridge of hills known as the Little Wolf Mountains. Mostly they had to feel their way, guided by the clink of mess cups in the unit ahead, and sometimes the horses turned back into the choking dust cloud, kicking, biting, the horse soldiers cursing their frustrations. Further back came the pack train, the braying of the foul-tempered mules clear as trumpet calls in the night. Back there, Captain Myles Keogh took out his anger on the civilian packers as some of the packs had come loose to splay out supplies. But he knew that to halt the unit he commanded would see them fall even further behind and chance being ambushed by the Sioux.

And there had been, away back before the Regiment had started on this night march, two Cheyenne warriors of Little Wolf's band viewing from deep cover some the younger officers celebrating their commander's decision to engage the Sioux as quickly as possible by singing a few songs. Notably among them had been "Annie Laurie," and for Custer, "For He's a Jolly Good Fellow."

At the head of the column, Lieutenant Colonel Custer would have had mixed emotions had he known of the presence of those Cheyenne warriors. First of all, it would have told Custer he had no other options than to make this night march. There was also the criticism voiced by some of his senior officers over their commander's decision not to continue on down the Rosebud and hook up with Crook. The most cutting voice had been Bloody Knife's, the Boy General's favorite scout, warning him in blunt language just what lay ahead. There were other voices adding to the murmur of Custer's thoughts; starry-eyed Autie Reed's, and Boston's, and the one he loved most of all — Libbie's. That musically soft voice of the woman he'd married caused his eyes to mist — but most probably it was a sudden gust of wind that flung back the stifling dust.

It came onto one o'clock , the half-hour, the sky darker as a few clouds rolled in to blot out stars. Even Custer rode with a bandanna drawn up over his mouth and nose, while behind him the Regiment had stretched out even more, with units pulling up to halt and listen, just to catch the direction of those ahead. Some of the companies meandered blindly into box canyons and were forced to turn back on themselves as if a rattler bellying away from danger. Horses whickered their anguish when they stepped into badger holes or stumbled over a washout and went down, their riders clutching desperately to the reins.

More than anything, for the young recruits venturing for the first time into Indian country, there was a dread of this night and the trail they were following — a trail cut and gouged nearly a half-mile wide down the Rosebud, the veterans with them picking up on fresh sign left by the Sioux at each sudden twisting of the valley floor. The fear of being attacked from ambush kept many a young soldier from falling asleep in the saddle.

Up where the dust was thinnest, the southwest wind sweeping it back over the Regiment, an angry Custer had ordered the Crow scout and Girard to ride on ahead — only to have them report back with disturbing news.

Said the Crow, Half Yellow Face, "It is a more difficult way ahead — there is a narrow, rocky passageway that will take us to the headwaters of another creek."

Around a grimace Custer asked, "How far from there to this ... Crow's Nest ..."

"Not all that far," said Girard. "Three, four miles. But we will be doing some climbing."

"Can't be helped," said Custer, whereupon he signaled for Lieutenant Cooke to come up, and as Custer uncorked his canteen, he asked him, "How does it look back there?"

"Dust's too thick to really determine how the companies

are faring, sir."

"Pass the word, Lo'tenant, that farther up it'll be single file." Through the sounds of confusion coming from behind him, Custer could make out the distant braying of a mule, a comforting sound, for it meant the pack train was keeping pace. Still, the way his Regiment was stretched out, it was vulnerable to attack. A risk — but there was the glory to the victor. More wearily, he ordered, "Pass the word."

By sheer determination Custer forced his Regiment on after the Sioux. Over terrain enshrouded with the pale, uncertain light of night, on to three, and then four o'clock. And now at a much slower gait.

Of them all, only Crow scout Half Yellow Face knew that the worry for the horse soldiers wasn't so much their angry curses or muted commands or the creaking of saddles but that any Lakota could feel the cadence of their passing simply by laying his palm to the bare earth. The Crow rode ahead of everyone, somewhat reluctantly, troubled by what he had known even before the pony soldiers had left Fort Abraham Lincoln — that the mighty Teton Lakota had been forewarned to the coming of the Yellow Hair.

But his mission, like that of the other scouts, was simply to bring the horse soldiers to the Lakota. So in the way of the Crow, Half Yellow Face knew he had not violated any trust. He pulled up on a crumbly elevation to look back at the Regiment. He took in Custer, the tireless man his soldiers called "Iron Bottom," shorn of the familiar golden locks, that big gelding Custer rode still with a spring in his gait. What more could he say to a man who'd ignored all of the signs left along the trail by the Lakota? In his heart, Half Yellow Face knew the wiser course was to remain silent. Then Girard came up, and with both men reining on, the Crow remarked that both of them might see another sunrise.

At this moment Custer, having been joined by the news hawk Mark Kellogg, realized that in just a couple of days the Democratic Convention opened in St. Louis. Refreshed by Kellogg cracking a chipper smile, he said, "Do you still feel you've hitched a ride with the right star?"

"General, yonderly I gather is the morning star." He gestured easterly, looked again at Custer. "A good omen, I'd say. A lot of scandals swirling around Grant, too. Oh, for a fact, General, your star is rising."

* * * * * *

In the grayness touching upon a vague sky rippling with clouds, the leading elements of the 7th Cavalry broke out of a rocky defile, spreading out over a flattish bottom under a high bluff. The horses neighed their thirst at a thin tendril of creek and the stinking pools comprising upper Davis Creek. Only to have a trooper shout out, "Damn ... nothing but alkaline!"

Custer reined his mount, Vic, through sagebrush more felt than seen in the lifting darkness. His staff officers came up as he swung a tired leg over the horse's rump and touched a boot upon pebbly ground. Around the small contingent of officers swirled the first of twelve companies of the Regiment, the heavy and raspy breathing of their horses filling the night air, as did the anxious commands of non-coms and officers.

Came Lieutenant Cooke's phlegmy voice, "Sufficient to say, gentlemen, my lungs and gullet are caked with dust." Through an amused smile showing even rows of teeth, he made a show of beating the dust from his goatee. "So we, I estimate, have ridden nine or ten miles. But to where?"

"Ten, according to the Crow." Custer knew they weren't all that far from the Crow's Nest. Beyond that rocky promontory lay the valley of the Little Big Horn. His spirits lifted, and, doubtful thoughts. In all probability the Sioux would be camped west of the river, or — he gritted his teeth, spat particles of dust out of his mouth — they'd pulled out.

From up-valley came a rider bearing a guidon, an abbreviated version of the national flag, two circles of stars on a field of blue, and with bars of red and white. The next horseman was Captain Tom Custer, who, upon sighting his brother, whistled a few notes from the Regimental song, "Garry Owen." Captain Tom's C Company troopers followed their leader heading further along the creek.

More companies pulled in through the defile just to the northeast. They were hard on the eastern flanks of the Little Wolfs, Custer having other concerns at the moment than the tired men and horses of his command.

He said, "There'll be no fires; understood? Spread the word." There was a slight stutter as he added, "My ... scouts, what have they found out ...?"

Photograph of a drawing by Chief Red Horse, a Lakota Miniconjou at the
Battle of the Little Bighorn (the Greasy Grass), of some of the numerous
lodges in the huge Native-American encampment prior to the battle.
Photo courtesy of The Smithsonian Institution.

Mitch Bouyer, a member of the Crow Nation, and one of Custer's scouts. Photo courtesy of the Denver Public Library, Western History Collection, picture taken by Charles A. Nast, apparently between 1875 & 1876. Call Number: X-31214.

CHAPTER 9

Curly: Some Fearful Medicine

Earlier the scouts commanded by Lieutenant Charles Varnum had found a curious arrangement of stones and buffalo skulls. It had been explained to Varnum this clearly indicated to the Lakota that they would have a great victory. Here they'd taken the time to smoke, the Ree and Crow scouts along with Curly.

Upon gazing at the message left by the Lakota, some of Curly's fears had resurfaced, as of a wolverine running over one's grave. He refrained from the quiet talk made by the others. The other white man, Lonesome Charlie, also held apart, but that was his way. The small point of light in the bowl of the pipe drifted from hand to hand. There was no need to hurry, since their destination was just beyond the next rise.

The lack of sleep didn't seem to bother the scouts, or the half-blood Bouyer. But that Varnum was overly tired showed in the way he was fighting to keep his eyes open. To counteract his tiredness he gave the order to move out, with one of the scouts dousing the pipe and stowing it away. From here they climbed aboard their horses to head up the eastern flank of a rocky hill in the Little Wolfs.

It was, by anyone's reckonings, sometime around three when they ghosted into the pocket the Crows had described.

While the others and Varnum settled in to catnap, Hairy Moccasin and Curly climbed on foot to the peak of the Nest.

Making himself comfortable, Curly murmured, "The stars seem closer. How they sparkle."

"They are not as plentiful as the Lakota."

Curly nodded, the excitement he felt shining in his eyes. He unslung the bow and quiver to lay them by his rifle. Together they gazed westerly into the Little Big Horn, but at this hour the floor of the valley still did not reveal the secrets it held. The storm which had been traipsing in from the Southwest had veered away. But still it muted far away rolls as there came thunderclaps, and jagged bolts piercing out of the blacker belly of the storm. The night, as it was doing for Custer and his Regiment, seemed to hold forever. And though Hairy Moccasin snugged down and closed his eyes, Curly knew his friend wasn't sleeping.

Through their only field glass they took turns as it cleared more to study the way of it further to the west. Soon it was Curly's younger eyes that picked up what the night had concealed, as he exclaimed, "Tipis across the river!"

Hairy Moccasin took his turn with the glass. Soon came his urgent, "Come." He lifted from the rocky ground to ease down the slope, where he cupped a hand to his mouth.

There was a stirring below when the Ree heard the soft cry of an owl, and they started singing their death songs.

Varnum snapped, "Enough of that." Scratching at his chin, he sighted in on Hairy Moccasin holding by a scattering of junipers, and he went upslope, to have Hairy Moccasin point back to the east where blued smoke issued from regimental campfires.

"Does Yellow Hair think those we seek have white-man eyes?"

Nodding impatiently, Varnum said, "What have you got?"

"Tipis and many horses," said Curly, "far west along the Greasy Grass." He handed the field glass to Varnum, with Curly and the others fanning out behind Varnum treading toward the Nest.

Here everyone bellied down. The others having field glasses were Bouyer and Lonesome Charlie Reynolds, and they quickly scoped-in on what the Crow scouts had discovered.

Only for Varnum this was proving to be hard to do because mist still webbed along the river. He figured they were at least eight miles out, the valley a series of sharp ridges and draws.

Off to Varnum's right Lonesome Charlie said matter-of-factly, "Got to be the biggest horse herd I've ever set eyes on ..."

"Far too big," amended the half-blood, Bouyer.

"Are you sure?"

Bouyer glanced at the lieutenant and said, "Pony herd looks like tangles of fish worms."

"Many, many tangles," Curly intoned.

But puzzlement was still etched to Varnum's wind-scoured face as his eyes, tired and bloodshot from almost three days of being saddlebound, kept him from focusing in on what the others were glimpsing, though he knew they'd found the Lakota from the excited pitch of voices around him. He gazed past Curly at a Ree, Red Star, to crook an urgent finger. Then he fumbled out some paper, a stub of pencil, to scribble a hasty note to Custer telling what they'd found. Handing the note to the Ree, Varnum said, "You, Bull, you go to ... tell Custer what we found."

The scouts left, Bull with the verbal message and heading out on his fresher horse, the Ree tending to the ritual of tying his horse's tail up in the sign of war before heading out.

The rest held to the Crow's Nest, letting the morning come to them, shedding fragrant thoughts of last night's dreams, drawing apart a little in uneasy contemplation of what this new day would bring — victory or death.

It was Curly, slipping down to relieve himself near some

sheltering junipers, who honed in on at least a half-dozen Indians coming out from cover to head east. Two of their bunch, whom Curly believed were Lakota, vanished into a dry coulee that cut in ahead of Red Star and Bull making for Custer's camp. Spinning around, Curly loped upslope to bring the news to Varnum.

"I'm sure they were Lakota."

"The luck of it all," groused Varnum. "What, ride after them? But that'll mean gunfire...betray our presence to the Sioux." He had moved down some to keep from being skylined, Lonesome Charlie in next to him, the scouts ready to break down for their mounts if the order came. But Lieutenant Varnum held them there, with everyone keening their ears for the sound of gunfire.

Barely able to contain his worry, Varnum fingered out his watch. "A little after five. Custer'll be up."

Corrected Bouyer, "Custer never sleeps." He turned with the others to labor up to the Nest, where they settled down to keep watch over the western reaches of the Little Big Horn.

Curly thought about the smallish river running cold and clear beyond the distant tree-line and the bluffs, a river flowing through horseshoe bends and next to a broad floodplain. Numberless times he had ridden along the Greasy Grass still deep with the waters of late spring as it lay in the lands of his people, the Crow. More to himself than to Hairy Moccasin and the nearby Bouoyer he said, "It will be hot — and a good day to die."

Chief American Horse, Dakota
Studio portrait of head and shoulders of American Horse, Dakota Chief,
wearing war bonnet and decorated vest.
Photograph by D.F. Barry, 1883
Photo courtesy of The Denver Public Library, Western History Collection,
Call number: B-164

Thomas McDougall (McDougal, M'Dougall) of B Troop.
As a captain in 1876, he was in charge of the Seventh Cavalry's
pack train at Little Bighorn.
Photo courtesy of The Denver Public Library, Western History Collection,
taken by D. F. Barry (1885),
Call Number: B-46.

CHAPTER 10

Custer: The Morning Star

No longer could the morning star be seen in the sky east of the 7th Cavalry trailing after Custer. With the arrival of the scouts, and the news the Sioux had been sighted, a new spirit gripped everyone, knowing that at last they would come to grips with the enemy. As for Custer, he held Vic to a walk, letting the slowing rising heat chase away the chill of the night.

When the scout had arrived with Varnum's message, it had been George Armstrong Custer leaping onto the first horse at hand to gallop bareback through the command, rousing his officers with orders they were to pull out within the hour.

Elation still rode with Custer, clad in a blue-gray flannel shirt and buckskin trousers, and broad whitish hat, at his neck the familiar red scarf picked out by Libbie. Here they were more on the eastern hills of the mountain than in the Rosebud Valley. Even at a walk dust rose uncontained to a high sky windrowed with a few clouds.

After the passage of about an hour the Regiment passed into a deep and heavily-wooded ravine. To the east the sun was stalking away from the horizon to burn down at a land that never seemed to receive enough rainwater. In evidence were some cutbanks, higher up chimney rock, everything shrouded by gritty dust stinging at red-rimmed and tired eyes.

Anxiously Custer swung his gelding around and picked out his taller adjutant. "Everyone will settle in here until I get back."

With a salute for his commander's eager, mustachioed smile, First Lieutenant W.W. Cooke relayed the order to a first-sergeant and nearby officers. Then Cooke wheeled his horse aside to find the shade of an ash. Reining in under the tree, he took a last look at Custer and Half Yellow Face and the interpreter Girard laboring their horses over a rise.

Adjutant Cooke was a troubled man, some of it caused by a quiet conversation he'd had last night with Custer, in that Custer meant to divide his command. He mused darkly: surely George Custer has to realize his command had been mentally divided long before we saw the Rosebud. There was Reno's disloyalty, in that he wants command of the 7th. There was acid-minded Benteen, hating Custer so much Lord knows what'll happen out there today, in the valley of the Little Big Horn.

Another worry, and of a deeper concern: Custer's deciding ever since we cleared the Yellowstone of a "reconnaissance-in-force." And they had. The Regiment advanced cautiously, gathering information as it went down the Rosebud, trying as he pushed his horses and men to the limits of their endurance to keep the segments of his command within functioning distance. Now comes the battle, heading out on trail-weary horses to take on, accordingto the scouts, the largest gathering of Indians the Great Plains had ever seen.

"I'm afraid it'll take more than Custer's luck …"

* * * * * * * *

Around dawn the sky had cleared, the new light of day at the backs of those viewing the Lakota encampment from the Crow's

Nest. Now with the sun hanging over his shoulder, the Boy General found his distant view of what he sought obscured by a wavering haze caused by the summer heat.

With some irritation he said, "I've been on the Plains a good many years. My eyesight is excellent. But … beyond the river … you claim there are Indian ponies …"

Without benefit of his field glass he tried piercing the shadowed heights and hollows of the valley, beyond to what his scouts said were also many lodges. He was down on one knee, and hatless, Custer was brushing an errant mosquito away. Close to him, Lonesome Charlie Reynolds refrained from pointing out what he could plainly see. But not so the half-blood Bouyer, as his voice came cutting through the rising heat of this Sunday morning in late June, "If you don't find more Indians than any of us ever saw before beyond the river, then you can hang me."

"All … right," stuttered Custer, "it would do no good to hang you."

The response from Custer did not erase the fears and anger of Mitch Bouyer, as he knew better than anyone the size and power of the Teton Lakota summer councils that had been driven from Bear Butte and the Black Hills by the miners. The same miners Custer's discovery of gold had brought there. Cuttingly he spoke again.

"Get your Regiment away from here as fast as your tired horses can carry you."

There was a vague nod from Custer as he brought the field glass to his eyes, still tucked down on one knee, to survey what he had been searching for. In him was this tug of expectancy, a rising excitement. For he realized something was churning up dust beyond the far reaches of the river. Lithely he rose and passed back Lonesome Charlie's glass, with his words directed to another.

"Varnum, hold here and keep watch. When we head into the valley, join my command."

* * * * * * *

On their way down the eastern slope the three of them, Custer, Girard, and Half Yellow Face, took in a cavalryman cantering his horse toward them from about where they'd left the Regiment. This time Custer's eyesight was keener.

"My brother, Captain Tom?"

They came together at the bottom of the slope and near brush flowing into a gully, where Tom Custer reined up his winded and sweating horse and said, "Seems some Indians have been following us after all, Autie. They found some hard bread boxes we lost."

"The luck of it all," Custer said grimly. That he was troubled showed in the way he spurred easterly to have the others play catch-up. Though he slowed down a little when Tom Custer drew alongside.

He threw at Tom, "Seems we've found them, camped the other side of the valley."

A pleased grin squinted Captain Tom Custer's eyes.

"Proves out a night march was the right decision. But they know we're here. Right now they could be breaking camp, just when we had them in the palms of our hands."

"You must know," said Tom Custer, "that Reno has brought along some whiskey. The point is, is he capable of command …?"

"He wanted to command the 7th," Custer shot back as they brought their horses down an angling slope and toward his command settled in amongst trees. He rode directly toward his guidon and the waiting Adjutant Cooke and Trumpeter John Martin, his bugler for the day. Sharply he called for assembly as he swung down, to have bugle notes pierce below the bluff and down a ravine.

He waived away the offer of Cooke's canteen, as there came this strange anxiety. It had come last night, during the few moments of sleep he'd allowed himself, a sharp remembrance of the message found in one of the sweat lodges.

Those painted rocks lined up in two rows, and what the Sioux scout had told him it meant — SOLDIERS FALLING INTO

CAMP. Too, there'd been the warning from Bloody Knife, and within the hour Mitch Bouyer's outburst up at the Crow's Nest. A spell, the Sioux scout had gone on to say, had been put upon the valley of the Little Big Horn by the Great Spirit.

The Boy General's lips curled in disdain. Nothing but sorcery practiced by Indian Shamans, had no place on a battlefield. There came visions of a glorious victory. And now an impatient gritting of his teeth, the officers coming in too slowly, a wisp of a headache touching his forehead.

"Hurry up now," he called out, to have him ease into the shade of a tree, his officers clustering around, some of them beginning to realize they were about to go into battle.

"Each company commander," Custer began, "is to select one non-commissioned officer and six privates from his troop and detail them to the pack train ... each man to lead two of the pack mules. As for what we found beyond the hills ..."

There was an exchange of wondering glances, for about their commander was a radical departure from the usual calm demeanor, this hesitancy of speech, the uncertainty sparking out of the deep-set eyes.

More vigorously now, "My scouts report they've sighted-in on a large Sioux camp just across the Little Big Horn River. But we've been spotted ..."

From where he stood by Benteen, Major Reno said quickly, "If so, General, we must not attack until tomorrow. At which time Crook ..."

"By then, Major Reno, there won't be any Indians for us to fight," lashed out Custer. He had not seen the need to reveal to anyone in his command the written orders he'd received from General Terry. In them was a loophole which gave Custer carte blanche to use his own judgment, and which read: "unless you see sufficient reason for departing from them." So at the moment sufficient reason for Custer consisted of the Indians lurking along his back-trail, the main encampment of the Sioux but a few hours' march away.

"Each commander will inspect his troop to satisfy himself that men and horses are ready for any contingency."

An eager smile for his officers, Custer added, "The troops will march in the order their commanders report them ready."

To Lieutenant Colonel George Custer's chagrin this honor soon fell upon Captain Benteen's H troop. Within minutes, other company commanders came back to report to the Regimental commander, the companies forming into the proper order of march. Custer's impatient mood brought Vic stomping and wheeling around in a tight circle, as Custer took in the last of his company commanders loping in, Captain McDougal of B troop.

"McDougal, you'll guard the pack train."

"But, sir, the pack train isn't ready to move out."

"When it does move out. Your troopers'll be guarding it," he threw over his shoulder.

And then with a wave of his arm the Boy General brought his command into motion.

George Armstrong Custer, as a Major-General.
Photo courtesy of The Library of Congress.

Major-General George Armstrong Custer
leads his Cavalry across the plains to the Black Hills.
Photo courtesy of The Library of Congress.

CHAPTER 11

Custer Leads His Regiment

The morning sun over his shoulder, Custer led his Regiment across the heavily traveled saddle of the divide and into the valley of the Little Big Horn. A few miles back, Benteen's H company had been out front, but setting too brisk a pace for Custer's liking. A halt had been ordered, with Custer drawing apart to consult with his adjutant.

Here he mulled over what he had told him before, realized it wasn't twenty or so miles from his present position, just south-westerly of the Crow's Nest and the Little Wolfs, but a far less distance to those trees stubbling along the river.

"What do you make of it, Cooke, more in the neighborhood of eight, nine miles?"

"About that."

They were gazing northwesterly, the lowering valley floor pointing like a rifle barrel at trees concealing the camp of the Sioux. To their right, the valley was one ridge after another, opposite higher hills stippled with jackpines and junipers and layers of greenish rock. They would guide on Ash Creek, which Custer's scouts had told him formed into three branches a few miles ahead and then plunged down bluffs into the Little Big Horn River.

When they moved on again, it was in a column of fours.

Shortly thereafter, Lieutenant Varnum and his scouts arrived, and again Custer halted his command, then to confer with Varnum.

"General, we observed some Indians breaking up camp and moving downstream."

Grimacing, Custer said, "What I feared most."

Mitch Bouyer warned, "There are far too many Lakota."

The Ree, Bloody Knife, nodded in agreement.

His voice tinged with frustration, Custer said, "Bouyer, you seem to be afraid."

The scout replied, "If we go in there we will never come out."

Bloody Knife strengthened this by gazing sunward to gesture in the sign-language of the Plains, his way of bidding farewell to the sun, and as he did this, he muttered to it, "I shall not see you go behind the hills tonight."

Custer spun his gelding away, an arm-signal fetching his command after him. He brought them along Ash Creek, the scouts fanning in front a short distance. Water in the smallish creek overflowed in some places, whereas in normal years the creek would be dried-up. Every so often Custer's penetrating eyes would go beyond the bluffs where his scouts believed the Sioux were encamped to powdery dust clogging the morning sky. If they are moving out, he mused, some of the braves are dragging branches across the floodplain to make a smokescreen. He wanted to pick up the pace, but there were the horses. He knew too, that only last night's march had brought them this close. With Reno commanding they would still be away back in the Rosebud, to let either Crook or Gibbon gain the glory. Another half-mile and further west along the creek brought a company command from Custer to halt. He motioned Cooke over, said quietly, "you tell Benteen I want him to take companies H, D, and K, and swing to the southwest at about forty-five degrees. I want Benteen to explore that line of bluffs."

"It was my impression, General," Cooke said hesitantly, "that Major Reno would command one element of the Regiment, you the main body…"

"Relay my order," Custer said stoically. As the adjutant reined back along the column, Custer's eyes went to his nephew, Autie Reed, chatting with Mark Kellogg, and next to him the corporal holding Custer's personal guidon. Should he send them back to the pack train? Perhaps Autie, as he desperately needed the newshawk's impression of the upcoming battle.

The battle. Must move out despite the fact that a lot of men had dismounted to give their tired horses all the rest they could. Let them rest later — after his 7th had severely whipped Sitting Bull, Crazy Horse, Gall, and their superior force. He thought about Boston Custer back with the pack train, recalled his promise that Boston could ride with his gray troop once hostilities commenced. Then, rising a gauntleted hand, he got the Regiment on the move again.

They were keeping north of Ash Creek. It was a lot hotter now, the sun creeping ever upward, with Custer glimpsing Benteen's column wending below some bluffs. He swung Vic sideways, waved chief trumpeteer Voss over, to issue instructions that Benteen was to continue on to the next line of bluffs if he found nothing on reaching the first. Further along, his call brought the Regimental sergeant-major up, Custer with further orders that Benteen, now lost to view, was to go on to the valley, and on and on.

More puzzled than dismayed by the Regimental commander's orders regarding Captain Benteen, Adjutant William Winer Cooke suddenly realized the reason's behind Custer's rash move. The Boy General would not let a man he loathed share his glory.

"Benteen's been sent chasing a wild trumpet, sent on a fool's errand."

This despite the chilling fact the Regiment was heading to

do battle with thousands of hostile Indians. And despite the heat, over his tiredness, Cooke shivered inwardly. He heard the barked command of "Left oblique," and twisted in the saddle to discover that three more companies were pulling out of the column: A, G, and M. In charge of them was Major Marcus Reno, jumping his horse across the narrow creek. From here to parallel the westward progress of the six companies still under Custer's direct command.

On they went on trail-weary horses, the creek twisting some and narrow at stretches where the troopers in the two detachments easily talked backed and forth. The morning wore on, on to around eleven, Custer straining to see over the rising ground and outcroppings of weathered sandstone sprinkled around the valley. Again he halted the Regiment when some scouts came riding back to report that off in the distance they were being observed by a small body of Indians. Just ahead, Ash Creek split into three forks, and there were mud-holes and reeds marking swampy places, with Custer spurring on to hook up with the scouts.

On an elevation, he sighted in on the few Indians, and saw that they were keeping just out of carbine range, and he said, "Go after them."

The mixture of Ree, Sioux, and Crow scouts held there, refusing to swing their horses about, and Custer said harshly, "If any of you is not brave, I will take away his weapons, and make a woman of him."

A Ree cried out, "Tell him if he does the same thing to all of his white soldiers who are not as brave as we, it will take him a long time indeed. This brought laughter from the scouts, an angry Custer breaking back to his command, and firming his decision to send Reno's battalion on the attack. From behind there came another sally from one of the Ree that there were more Lakota ahead than there were bullets in the belts of the soldiers.

Immediately upon reining up, Custer spoke quietly but decisively to his Adjutant, Lieutenant Cooke in the presence of his orderly, Trumpeter John Martin. Whereupon Cooke, as Custer held there, broke off to the south where Major Reno was waiting just across the narrow expanse of creek. Splashing through the shallow water, he pulled up and said, "Major, orders from General Custer are for you to take your three troops … cross the river … and attack the Indian camp from the south. Custer will support with the rest of the command."

"We're not certain just how many hostiles are down there, Cooke," said Reno. "I don't like this idea of splitting our forces."

"The Indians, Major, seem to be running away."

"At least we've got them on the run."

"You're to move forward at as rapid a gait as you think prudent."

Major Marcus Reno took in the dusty haze beyond the bluffs guarding the floodplain and said bluntly, "As prudent a pace; our horses can barely keep to a canter. This will take a little time. As once we hit the river its damned necessary we water our horses, let them rest. Then … I expect you'll hear gunfire …"

"One other thing," said Cooke, "the scouts will go with your command. And, sir, good luck."

There was a searching look from Reno, a pursing of his lips, an abject nodding of his head as if he were reluctant to carry out his commander's order. "Luck — just make sure I get that support."

Henry rifle M1860, .44 caliber. Photo by Richard Strauss.

The Henry rifle was the immediate forerunner of the famous Winchester rifles. About 14,000 Henry's were made between 1860 and 1866 by the New Haven Arms Company. The Henry rifle was developed from the Volcanic firearms system and was built around the .44 rimfire cartridge. Both the new rifle and the cartridge were designed by B. Tyler Henry. A basic feature of the .44 rimfire cartridge was the use of a metallic casing, rather than the undependable, self-contained powder, ball, and primer of the Volcanic bullet. Evidence indicates that the Indians at Little Big Horn had a large number of Henry rifles, while the Army was armed with the single-shot breechloading Springfield Model 1873.

Photo & description courtesy of The Smithsonian Institution

Springfield Carbine M1873, .45 caliber.

The Springfield carbine was the classic gun of the Old West. It was designed to use a new more powerful .45 caliber government cartridge. The legendary 7th Cavalry received the first shipment in June 1874 to replace the old Civil War Sharps and Spencer carbine. By 25 June 1876 most of General George Custer's troops were armed with the Springfield M1873 when they were overrun at the Little Bighorn.

Photo & description courtesy of The Smithsonian Institution.

Smith & Wesson First Model Schofield revolver, .45 caliber. U.S. Army.
This Smith & Wesson was found loaded at the
Little Bighorn Battlefield in 1883.

Photo courtesy of the Smithsonian Institution

The gun in <u>front</u> of the box is a Second Model Smith & Wesson Schofield
revolver. The guns that are <u>in</u> the box are the First Model,
the same as those used by Custer's troops at the Battle of the Little Bighorn.

Courtesy of Roy G. Jinks, Smith & Wesson Historian

Major Marcus A. Reno
Photo courtesy of the Denver Public Library, Western History Collection,
photograph by D. F. Barry (taken sometime between 1874 & 1876),
Call Number: B-603.

CHAPTER 12

Reno

Even Adjutant Cooke's parting words to him that Captain Benteen would support his left flank couldn't dislodge the doubts felt by Major Marcus Reno bringing his battalion along the south fork of Ash Creek. More, it had rankled him that Custer hadn't had the decency to give him his orders directly. Perhaps it was just as well, as there might have been an exchange of words.

Reno took note of the fact that most of the scouts were hanging on at the head of the column, and that four Crow scouts and Mitch Bouyer were still with Custer. And it was just like George Custer to have that reporter and that nephew of his go in harm's way. As without question Reno knew that within the next couple of hours, or even sooner, blood would be spilled along the Little Big Horn.

"The Gatling guns," Reno thought, "should have taken them along. The audacity of Custer turning down Gibbon's offer of three companies! Could prove to be a deciding factor." His dark, brooding eyes squinting away from the dust and sun, he knew that by rights the Regiment should be his to command.

Only to have Terry snatch it away from him up at the Yellowstone.

"Damnable heat," he cursed, and with Reno acutely in need of the whiskey packed along in his canteen. There'd been a time in his life when whiskey had been of little importance. But after all the disappointments, then to be assigned to the 7th and be under the command of a man he despised. Only the presence of Captain Benteen, and of others in the Regiment with a naked dislike of Custer, and the whiskey, had made it bearable.

Following close to Reno were Lieutenant Wallace, recorder for the Regiment, and Reno's adjutant, Lieutenant Hodgson. The initial excitement of the men close enough to overhear the orders from Custer, and which had been relayed from company to company, had been replaced by worry of what lay ahead — ahead on the wide, worn lodge trail following the twisting creek and stagnant pools. Off to the right Custer's column could still be seen, the only indication the pack train was far behind in the valley, the faint cloud of dust. Now through a cut those out front glimpsed the crowns of trees fringing along the Little Big Horn River, the gait picking up slightly.

* * * * * * * *

Somewhat reluctantly, their rifles ready, the scouts were the first to urge their horses down through the cutbank. Among the first to reach the riverbank was Bloody Knife, who reined upriver just a little before he let his horse drink, most of the other scouts coming in around him.

Cottonwoods sent down a little shade, the brush and trees thicker across the river, and like the others, Bloody Knife expected to be fired upon at any moment.

Down came the horse soldiers, cursing as they tried to control their mounts catching the scent of water, with some of the horses taking the bit and jumping into the river to slake their thirst. In the confusion more troopers emerged from the cutbank, the sergeants and officers shouting for control. While here the river ran swift and deep, at least thirty feet from bank to bank.

"Don't let them drink too much. Else they'll die right under your saddle!"

"Keep away from the high bank!"

"You, McDonald, get back from there!"

"This might be your last change to fill your canteens, so tend to it!"

Further up the cutbank a horse went down, pitching its rider forward to hit the gravelly ground. A non-com was there to grab the reins as the horse lurched to its feet, the non-com screaming at the private to reclaim his mount.

Soon the trailing edges of the battalion were spreading out along the river, when Reno was told of a natural ford just downstream. He looked to the north wiping sweat from his face, and at the way the river went ox-bowing until it was hidden by screening brush. Above this fortress of brush, the trees stood motionless, seeming to be waiting for something to happen. Down in here between the bluffs and the river the heat seemed to be contained, but at least, mused an apprehensive Marcus Reno, they had drinking water.

To Bloody Knife who'd just walked his horse over he said, "How far up is that Indian camp?"

"Close, a mile, maybe two."

"Check out that crossing." Then Reno was issuing more orders not heralded by trumpet calls, an order for M Company to go after Bloody Knife, some scouts to tag along. He swung into the saddle even as he looked about for the few officers he knew were veteran Indian fighters, as he wanted them close at hand. But there was still too much confusion, the three companies spread out thinly along the riverbank.

Now he directed his attention to one of the Crow scouts recrossing to the east bank, to announce that the Lakota were coming to meet them.

"Head 'em across!" Reno shouted, as he spurred downriver and to find Bloody Knife. He pointed back at the cutbank, shouted accusingly, "Some of your Arikara scouts are refusing to cross the river."

"All my people hired on to do was to bring you to the Lakota. They go now."

"I can't have this," Reno said desperately to the first stirrings of fear. Around him another company was following M company's advance across the river at the natural crossing, and Reno realized he had no choice but to do the same.

He left behind Lieutenant Varnum swinging his horse about and heading back to the cutbank, where he shouted his contempt at the Ree, "Are you women? The enemy is there — across the river!

"Here, Girard, tell them what I said!"

Now the interpreter began haranguing the Ree in their own language, until finally about a dozen of them broke toward the ford to plunge their horses across the river. As Girard headed toward the ford, Varnum tarried just long enough to glare at the rest of the Arikara urging their mounts up the cutbank.

Across the river, the business of sorting out the confusion was taking place, both horses and men grateful for the brief chance to take on fresh water, yet at the same time realizing to a man that they were closing in on a vastly superior force. Reno's voice cracked as he gave the order to move out in columns of two. Out front with him were Lieutenants Varnum and Hare, with them Lonesome Charlie Reynolds and the Negro, Isaiah Dorman. The mixture of Ree and Sioux scouts were in close to the column. Hanging next to Reno rode Bloody Knife.

Reno kept his command close to the fringing of trees, right of them the crooked, tortuous river, westerly openness and rising, barren benchlands. The floodplain was empty, dotted with sagebrush, with just a whisper of wind snatching up powdery dust from the ground chewed by heavy use. They were conscious of the fact that at some distance ahead lay a thumb of brush and timber extending to the west. Beyond this low ridgeline rose massive dust clouds through which those out in front of the column could discern movement.

"What do you make of it? Their main camp?"

"Yessir, I . . ."

Reno swung away from Varnum and crooked an anxious finger that summoned his striker over, McIlhargy of Keogh's I Company. "Go and tell Custer I have everything in front of me and the enemy is strong." He watched the courier break back into the timber and to the southeast, Reno feeling that the Regimental commander had betrayed him, and then he spurred on to catch up with Varnum.

Back before leaving the river ford, Reno had formed two of his companies in fours, the third commanded by Lieutenant McIntosh holding back in reserve. Gauging where they were, Reno concluded they were about a mile from the low ridge-line, that it was time to move up faster, and he brought his battalion to a gallop. Though they tried, the horses were laboring, struggling to maintain the faster gait, while down the length of the column everyone was catching glimpses of Indians slinking southward through the brush. When he felt it was time, Reno gave the order that brought the pair of lead companies into line, the thin sweet notes of the a bugle swept away by the heavy thudding of hooves on the hard ground.

It was here that Reno changed his mind, caused by still more and more Sioux warriors riding his way out of the dust cloud obscuring the village, to have him bring the reserve company into line.

"Call charge!" he shouted. "Charge! Charge!"

The words came out of a mouth craving a drink, the fear

that he would receive no support from the rest of the Regiment. Nonetheless, he jabbed spurs to the sweating flanks of his horse. He was sweating profusely, scarcely able to suck in the dusty air, the horse quivering under him as he let it gallop closer to the low and screening ridgeline through which Sioux warriors were emerging, some of them veering toward the Arikara scouts making a go at the horse herd, more of the Sioux striking toward the trees in an attempt to turn Reno's right flank.

Out of Reno's eyes shone fear and uncertainties, a brief thought that perhaps he was overplaying his hand, then he gave the order to halt, and to dismount. Even as Reno's command brought everyone reining up, a few troopers were unable to stop their mounts. In fascinated horror, Reno watched the troopers on their runaway horses punching through Sioux warriors and then through the rising ridgeline, where they were instantly killed near the southern fringes of the vast encampment.

Now he was aware of a ragged volley of rifle-fire coming from his troopers, with Reno barking at a private firing a scant yard away, Trooper Mitchell, a cook, "You, head back across the river and tell Custer we've engaged hundreds of hostiles! Quickly, man!"

Without further hesitation the trooper vaulted into the saddle and was wheeling away to the south. Crouching now, Reno removed his straw hat as he took stock of the situation. He used the same hand to wipe sweat from his brow, glancing about, realizing that all he had were about ninety men forming a skirmish line of only a few hundred yards in length. Horse holders, one trooper for every four horses, had gone to the right to a track of a brushland lowering toward the river. Quartering to the north, and not over a hundred yards, hordes of mounted hostiles were coming at him through the swirling dust.

Around him came the pounding of gunfire, the acrid stench of burned powder, a look down the line to see men going down, blood splattering dusty uniforms and dirty white skin, the sight less eyes. Along with the screams of agony of the wounded, the yip-yapping of the attacking Indians, now someone screaming in Reno's ear that the line couldn't hold. Reno kept triggering his revolver seemingly without effect, then he realized it was Varnum, with more terrifying news that more of the Sioux were infiltrating along the river toward their horses.

Reno shouted, "Pull G company off the line," even as fear gaped his eyes, and as Varnum hurried away. Reno dropped to his knees and with shaking hands managed to cram some cartridges into his revolver as Captain Moylan appeared to inform Reno that the line was too thin.

"Major, our left flank's 'in the air.' We could be turned by the hostiles. Surrounded and cut to ribbons."

"What do you suggest …?"

"Withdraw to the timber and our horses." Moylan didn't hesitate as he turned away to issue the command to the trumpeter.

The bugle call and shouts from both Reno and Moylan brought the troopers falling back in orderly fashion to their right, more getting hit by erratic rifle-fire from the Sioux, who were sensing victory, and by their arrows. As best they could, the troopers positioned themselves amongst shrub trees and behind a cutbank left when the Little Big Horn had changed course to a new channel. There was still some confusion, as companies merged together in the entanglement of rose and plum brush growing thick around box elders, ash, cottonwood trees. The woods seemed to contain the heavy stench of black powder smoke augmented by heavier smoke coming from fires set downriver by the Sioux. And around them bullets screamed and ripped through green foliage, and men went down.

Reno, aware that the force before him was growing minute by minute, was reminded of the trail they'd first picked up on in the Rosebud — thousands of them, he realized. Too many, even for the whole Regiment.

Another danger was the diminishing visibility as the fire swept toward them, to lap eagerly at the brush, to send flaming embers lancing to set whole trees afire, the thickening smoke spilling in to frighten the seasoned cavalry horses. At the same time, closer to the river, the searing flames were driving troopers back to collapse Reno's makeshift defense.

Almost blindly Reno looked about, to spot Moylan firing away, with another officer, McIntosh, and he darted to them and said, "We've got to pull up to those bluffs before its too late!"

"We'd be naked up there!" objected Moylan.

"Our only chance!" shouted Reno, and as the pair of officers left to spread the word to the troopers, Reno sighted-in on Lonesome Charlie Reynolds calmly thrusting cartridges into the breech of his rifle, and closer to him, the Ree scout, Bloody Knife. Reno crouched over to Bloody Knife.

By sign-language he asked Bloody Knife where the next thrust from the Sioux would come. Grimacing in thought, the Ree lowered his rifle. This proved to be his last conscious act, as through the brush tore a volley of bullets, one of them punching into the Ree's head. The hard impact blew Bloody Knife's skull open as if it were an exploding melon, spilling blood onto the black silk handkerchief with blue stars presented to him by Custer, and more blood spattering across a horror-stricken Major Reno's face and shoulders.

As the Ree dropped, Reno lurched backwards, clutching his revolver and fighting down the bile and ghastly fear.

Out of this he managed to shout, "Pull back! Across the river to the bluffs! Pull back!"

Reno Ford of the Little Bighorn.
photographed by D. F. Barry in 1886 at the Reenactment of the Battle of Little
Bighorn taken on Tenth Anniversary and Reunion of the battle, June 26, 1886.
This shows the area where Reno first crossed the Little Bighorn River
and shows people and horses on the other side.
Photo courtesy of the Denver Public Library,
Call Number: B-810.

Rain In The Face (circa 1805 – 1905), a Hunkpapa Sioux chief.
(Picture taken between 1865 & 1880) source: Paul Harbaugh loan,
Rain In The Face was reputed by some to have been the warrior who killed
Custer, although there is considerable debate over who did.
Courtesy of the Denver Public Library,
Call Number: X-31695.

CHAPTER 13

Dust in the Sky

As dawn chased the night toward the western sky, the great encampment was already shaping this new day. Calls of greeting blended in with the bird songs as old ones voiced their pleasure at seeing another day. Young men walked or rode to see to their families' horses. Girls and young women made their way to the river with water flasks, some choosing a path that took them near the brush shelter of this or that unattached young warrior. Breezes wandered among the lodges, awakening a still-sleepy face with a soft touch and carrying the good smell of coffee and roasting meat. A gray pile of smoldering embers were the shrinking remains of a large fire in the Cheyenne camp, where Cheyenne and Lakota had danced the scalp dances far into the night. Small boys gathered here and there, reminding one another of plans concocted the previous evening, and anxious to answer the beckoning of this new day. And there was in the air something that was as yet unnamed, like the dark watcher ducking out of sight away from the searching glance.

111

Here and there in the camp, an old warrior sent a shrewd gaze toward the hazy distances of early morning, trying to corner an elusive feeling. Trying to glimpse the watcher, and not succeeding.

The soft orange streaks of dawn strengthened into bold red waves just before the sun jumped the eastern horizon, chasing the last stubborn vestiges of blue night shadows into the folds of departing night. Dawn turned itself into bright morning and the sun danced upward into the circle of the sky.

A man, slender as a youth, with waist-length brown hair wrapped with red cloth and otter skin, led a sleek bay horse as he walked toward the Cheyenne camp. Two eagle feathers hung downward at the back of his head. A long, wide border of quill-work, mostly in blues, with red and yellow, edged the sides of his tan deerhide leggings. The breech-clout was rubbed with blue and a narrow line of soft blue quills bordered his elk hide moccasins. His only weapons were a knife in its sheath hanging from the undecorated sash tied around the waist, and the repeating rifle in its beaded case carried in the crook of his left arm. A bullet bag hung at his right hip and in his right hand was a reddish-brown feather from the tail of a golden eagle.

At the southern end of the Cheyenne camp circle, the Oglala warrior stopped at a lodge decorated with the painting of a mounted hunter chasing a buffalo. Before the warrior could scratch at the door, an old woman emerged.

A hand went to her mouth as she recognized the man and whispered his name. "Crazy Horse."

"Grandmother," the warrior said, looking down at the dusty earth. "It is good to see you." A child and a young woman came out of the lodge behind the old woman. The young woman instantly recognized the slender, light-haired Lakota, but said nothing. Instead, she kept her eyes averted from the man's face, mostly out of a sudden shyness but also because it was the proper way. Her name was Buffalo Calf Road.

Even as the Oglala warrior slowly lifted the eagle feather toward the young woman, he could see her on her horse at the Rosebud fight. She had dashed through a hail of soldier bullets to rescue her brother, whose horse had been shot. A very strong, very brave thing to do. "Sister," Crazy Horse said softly. "It was an honor to have ridden against Three Stars' bluecoats with you. My other father, he who showed me the path of the warrior, gave me this feather, long ago. Now it is yours. I will never forget what you did there, at the Rosebud Fight. You have brought your family much honor." The young woman's hand trembled as she reached for the feather. Its base was wrapped in red. The honor color. She could hardly bring herself to believe the words she had just heard. Before she could find her voice to speak her appreciation, something else was in her hand, a soft, buffalo hair rope. The jaw rope of the sturdy little bay standing next to the Oglala warrior. Crazy Horse gently laid the coiled rope in her palm. "He is fast, and quick on his feet," he told her. "And he has the soul of a warrior."

Buffalo Calf Road could not speak. She struggled to keep back the tears. On this little bay, Crazy Horse had led the final charge at the Rosebud Fight, the final charge which broke the soldiers and brought victory for the Lakota and Cheyenne. She squeezed the rope and stared at the eagle feather. This moment was beyond any she could have imagined. A hand went quickly to the corner of her eye as she finally spoke, and that barely above a whisper.

"We are boiling some of the black medicine, coffee," she said. "Come and join us at our fire, and I will bring you food."

Crazy Horse ate and visited with the fine family of Buffalo Calf Road. Her brother, Comes in Sight, unselfishly told the story of his sister's brave deed to each new arrival who came to wonder about the sleek new bay picketed next to the family lodge. Many people came and stayed, but hung back politely. Many were seeing the glorious Oglala warrior for the first time ever. After a time, he spoke his thanks to Buffalo Calf Road and her mother, and went off to the lodge of Two Moons, leader of the Cheyennes. Along the way he paused to speak with a small boy who wanted to show him a new bow. A girl pushed her way through the crowd and placed a small bundle of sage in the warrior's hand, and then, yielding to shyness, dashed away.

At the lodge of Two Moons, Crazy Horse smoked with the Cheyenne and they talked of Sitting Bull's call for a council at sundown. At mid-morning the Oglala took his leave and made his way back to his own camp, stopping here and there to visit.

Southeast from the Cheyenne camp and east of the Sicangu circle, two young warriors finished watering their horses and returned to their brush shelter. They picketed their horses in some willows next to their small camp, and talked about their good fortune at meeting the great Hunkpapa medicine-man and being fed in his lodge. As they talked they also took the great man's parting advice to heart. White Feather Tail counted his war arrows and Bear poured his meager supply of bullets onto a hide and inspected each shell. All of the arrows were tipped with iron heads, iron from barrel hoops. Each head was sharp and those of the war arrows were attached horizontally, to pass between the ribs of an enemy warrior. Or a bluecoat soldier. The heads of hunting arrows were attached vertically, to pass between the ribs of elk, deer and bison. Though all arrows spun in flight and the arrow heads did not remain horizontal or vertical as they struck their targets, be it man or animal, each arrow nonetheless had specific purpose. For the warpath or for the hunt.

Bear, the slender one, finished inspecting his bullets and looked over at his cousin. Since boyhood, White Feather Tail had a particular fondness for the bow and arrow. Even to the point of passing on the gift of an old rifle to Bear. At each night camp on their journey from the Smoking Earth River to the great encampment, White Feather Tail worked on his arrows. And each dawn, before they resumed their journey, the broad-shouldered young

114

warrior practiced his marksmanship. At twenty paces he could easily hit a dry oak leaf. At forty paces, a sitting cottontail was as good as cooked. Then there was the three-arrows game. He would hold two arrows in the crook of the fingers of the bow hand and one notched on the string. With the bow up high, he would shoot the first arrow up and off into the distance. Before it hit the ground, the other two arrows were also hissing skyward. An old, old game. Played to sharpen the skills.

Bear gathered his bullets. "How many do you have now?"

White Feather Tail was fitting arrows into a holder and sliding it into the quiver. "Forty," he said. "And sixteen hunting arrows." He pointed at another bunch in a second quiver. "Turning Bear said something about going after elk in the Shining Mountains." He smiled in anticipation. "How many bullets do you have?"

"Eleven," was the disappointed reply.

"It would be good to keep the bow and arrows with you," the stocky warrior suggested to his cousin.

Bear smiled and put the bullets back into a bag. "I will do that," he assured his smiling cousin. "Yesterday I heard Big Road, the Oglala, talking to someone from the Itazipacola camp about the Rosebud Fight. He said a few men were able to capture some blue-coat rifles. But not many."

White Feather Tail nodded, and looked off to the north at the sudden sound of hoofbeats. Three young men were bringing horses to water. His cousin had not spoken of it — their disappointment at arriving too late to be part of the Rosebud Fight. But it was there, as real as anything in this encampment.

Two moons past, word had reached a small Sicangu camp along the Smoking Earth River. Sitting Bull, the Hunkpapa, had called for a gathering. "Along the Greasy Grass," the messenger had said. And he also brought word of Crazy Horse being made overall leader of the Oglala. It was enough. The two young Sicangu had decided to travel west. They had started in the Moon of the

Shedding Ponies. They would have walked, but a kind relative loaned them each a horse, Bear a black-and-white paint and White Feather Tail a buckskin. They had arrived at the great gathering while the camp was still on Ash Creek. The talk of the Rosebud Fight was in every lodge and around every fire. White Feather Tail learned that a distant Oglala relative, on his mother's side, had been wounded in the fight. Furthermore, young Black Wolf had carried the war leader's staff.

The cousins went from one warrior gathering to another, listening with envy to the stories recounted over and over again. They stood in the crowd at each scalp dance and watched as warriors were honored. Such things mellowed their disappointment, but did not chase it away entirely. This morning, for some reason, it had come back in a strong rush. White Feather Tail looked at the three young men with their horses, and wondered if they had been at the Rosebud Fight. An elk hunt in the Shining Mountains was not the same thing as a ride on the warpath. But it did have its own value. He would go with Turning Bear.

Just beyond a strong arrow cast from the small camp of the Sicangu stood the council lodge, larger than any in the encampment. Within, as the sun neared its mid-day point and sent down promise of a hot afternoon, several men ate together. Elk ribs roasted over the open fire was a great delicacy. Around the circle sat Black Moon, Crow King, and Sitting Bull of the Hunkpapa. Next to him was Kills Eagle of the Sihasapa. Rain in the Face, another Hunkpapa, had been a late arrival. After the meal, Sitting Bull politely convinced Kills Eagle to keep his people in the camp for another day or two. "I have asked for a Council at sundown," he said. "I know that we must all go away from here sooner or later. The grass will be eaten down and the deer and elk always know to move away from a large, hungry gathering. And we have things to do. Important things, like making meat for the coming winter." He paused to glance ever so briefly around the circle of faces. "But before we go, we must talk about another very important thing. This problem with the white man." The Hunkpapa medicine-man moved his hand in a wide slow circle. "We must all think alike and have the same way of dealing with the white man."

Every head nodded in agreement. An emphatic affirmation came from the lips of Rain in the Face. It was well known that no one had more hate for the white man than this Hunkpapa warrior. He had been taken in chains and held in a guard house at their Fort Abraham Lincoln. While there, imprisoned for an offense against white men that he did not commit, he was severely beaten by an army officer as other soldiers held the Hunkpapa's arms. To Rain in the Face, nothing in this life was more despicable than a white man.

Black Moon cleared his throat. "Uncle," he said to Sitting Bull. "Will you tell us of the Crow who was caught sneaking up on our camp?"

Heads swung around toward Black Moon, and then at the great medicine-man. Sitting Bull nodded. "Yes," he said. "I will tell you what I know."

Off to the west and a little north of the council lodge, Crazy Horse drew on his short-stemmed pipe and mulled over the news just brought to him. A young Oglala had overhead a conversation in the Hunkpapa camp. Words spoken quietly about an intruder captured by two Hunkpapa warriors sometime before dawn. A Crow warrior with a warning. Soldiers, coming from the Rosebud toward the Greasy Grass. Then the Crow had somehow managed to escape. Crazy Horse had sent the young messenger to the lodge of Big Road. This thing must be considered carefully.

Soldiers were in the country. That much was known. Reports had come down from the Yellowstone River area of soldier movements there. Soldiers could easily move down the Rosebud from the Yellowstone. Or perhaps Three Stars had turned around. Three Stars knew for certain that he had been attacked from the north or northwest. He would guess that the Lakota and Cheyenne were within striking distance from the battle site on Rosebud Creek. Still, recent reports had placed Three Stars near Goose Creek. That was south of where the battle had been fought. Crazy Horse doubted that Three Stars could push his army hard enough to be high on the Rosebud east of the Wolf Mountains.

The Oglala relit his pipe. In the end, it did not matter which group of soldiers would come. They all came with the same purpose. Whoever led them was unimportant. So was the direction of their approach. The important thing was to stop them. The threat of soldiers had been a part of Lakota life since the white began moving westward in greater and greater numbers. They were like the splinter which could not be dug from the finger. The white soldiers had shown their hearts at the Washita River and Sand Creek.

Those memories were fresh as yesterday for the Cheyenne. The Sicangu Lakota still remembered the Blue Water where Little Thunder's camp had been destroyed, and many people were killed. So, soldiers being here or there was not a surprising thing. It was that a Crow warrior, an enemy of the Lakota, would carry news of soldiers to the Lakota which was surprising. Crazy Horse looked up at the sound of soft rustling. The look of worry in his eyes softened into a smile. It was Black Shawl rolling up the sides of the lodge. The sun was hot and she wanted the breeze to cool the interior.

Big Road appeared, stooping to enter the lodge. "Cousin, do you know that some women and children are moving out of the camp?" he asked. Not waiting for a reply, he said, "Sometime this morning. Word is going around that a large group of bluecoats are close. They are going in groups to the west and north. Toward the hills. To hide, they said."

This was a new thing. Crazy Horse stood and followed Big Road out of the lodge. Even as the Oglala leader stood within his camp circle and gazed about at the activity around him, a rider far to the southeast was whipping his horse back toward the great encampment. Earlier, traveling east, he rode to the crest of a ridge and saw it. A great dust cloud hanging over the earth just beyond Ash Creek. And then he saw the dark shapes of men and horses beneath it.

He reached the Greasy Grass and plunged his horse in where there was no crossing. Up over the opposite bank he whipped the tired horse into gallop. As he approached some brush shelters near the edge of the large encampment, he began to shout.

"They are coming this way! Soldiers! Many soldiers!"

The alarm spread quickly from the Sihasapa and Itazipacola camps. It reached the council lodge like a sharp, hot gust of wind. Sitting Bull and the others came out quickly, to see what was taking shape. A young Hunkpapa ran up. "Someone has just ridden in! He says there is a dust cloud beyond the ridges to the east! And soldiers, many soldiers!"

So, it is to be this camp, Sitting Bull thought.

All around, the people were reacting to the alarm. Women, young and old, and older girls gathered up the children. Warriors hurried to their lodges to gather their weapons, some taking a moment to daub on war paint. Some were able to have a brief parting with their families. Others came back to empty lodges, hoping their families were away to safety. Old warriors grabbed their weapons, too. Some accompanied the women and children. They would be the last line of defense for the helpless ones. And others hurried toward the southeast, toward the lower end of the great encampment, hoping to be of some help in the coming fight. And the first far-away sounds of gunfire came from the southeast, from near the Hunkpapa camp circle.

Two Oglala, Crazy Horse and Big Road, exchanged hard, knowing glances. Without a word Big Road hurried away to his lodge. As the Oglala war leader turned, Black Shawl was already gathering his things. She held out his paint bag as he approached.

119

He took it. She waited, calm in the midst of noise and confusion all around, as he painted yellow hailstones on his chest and shoulders. When he finished, she handed him his rifle, bowcase and quiver of arrows, a warclub, and his shield. Finally she laid the jaw rope of the tan-and-white mare in his hands. He threw gopher dust on the horse and then tenderly pulled the woman to him.

"Perhaps you can go with the others," he said, nodding toward the northwest. "And find a place to hide."

Black Shawl pointed to a buckskin gelding tied to a branch. His second war horse for this day. "I will have him ready," she said. "If you should need him."

He lifted a hand to her chin, then turned to swing onto the mare. Such a wife was worth a warrior's death. Up on the prancing little mare, he rode through the Oglala camp.

"Come, my friends," he shouted. "These soldiers should not be here. It is time to send them to a different place."

Gall, the tall, handsome war leader of the Hunkpapa, was in between the Sihasapa and Miniconju camps when he heard the alarm. Then came the first sounds of gunfire. He turned his back but could not hurry through the sudden melee of people moving in every direction. A time or two the horse sidestepped children or dogs. The sound of bullets whining overhead began to come regularly. Near his own camp the confusion thinned out a little and he was able to lope the black toward his lodge. He came around a low clump of plum bushes and saw the bodies. Three of them. A woman and two children. Still. And lifeless. A sharp growl came up out of his chest when he recognized the woman's hairstrings. "Haun!" The dead bodies were his family.

He went to them and knelt close, touching each motionless form. Hoping for some sign of life. Some sign that none of what was happening was real. But none came. They were dead. Part of him believed it. Part of him would not. He looked off toward the east. Many warriors were already beyond the Hunkpapa camp.

Already meeting the advance of the bluecoats. Gunfire boomed and echoed through the river bottoms, and the shouts of soldiers and screams of horses could be heard. And above it all, a cloud of dust rose into the sky. Death had come through the dust in the sky, and wounded this Hunkpapa warrior in the deepest possible place.

Gall, the warrior who had unflinchingly faced Crow, Arikara, Blackfeet, and bluecoats, pulled his knife and sliced his shirt until it hung on him like tattered streamers. Then his forearms. As his own blood flowed, he rocked his body slowly. And wept.

White Man Runs Him
Photograph taken by Richard Throssel in 1913,
White Man Runs him was one of Custer's Crow scouts, and is a relative
of one of the authors of this book, Fred Lefthand.
Courtesy of the Denver Public Library,
Call Number: X-31261.

CHAPTER 14

Like a Lance Thrust Toward the Belly

Word of the attack finally reached the Cheyenne camp. By then, many Lakota women and children and old ones had reached the edge of the encampment to the west and north. There was confusion in the camp circles. Warriors raced to and from the horse herds. Old warriors wandered through the groups of people still in the camps, trying to calm the nerves of frightened women and children, shouting encouragement to the younger warriors.

The Cheyenne camp responded to the alarm, but as yet they could hear no gunfire or see any soldiers. Someone told them that the soldiers had ridden into the Hunkpapa camp. Those who had friends and acquaintances there were all the more frightened. Soon, groups of Cheyenne, women and children hurried to the west, after grabbing a little food and robes for the children in case they would need to spend the night in hiding.

Two Moons, the Cheyenne leader, gathered warriors to him. "Our friends need our help!" he shouted. He pointed to five or six warriors. "I must ask you to stand guard in our camp. I hope that the rest of you will follow me. We must not turn back from this enemy, even if we know we will die!" Two Moons turned his horse toward the Hunkpapa camp, the contingent of Cheyenne warriors close on his heels.

The soldiers had come down from the coulees and crossed at a ford just south of Ash Creek. By the time they came around a bend in the river and turned northwesterly, toward the lower end of the camp, many Lakota warriors were already converging beyond the Hunkpapa camp. Dust rose as the soldiers made their charge. Their first shots ripped through the lodges on the south-eastern edge of the Hunkpapa circle.

It was hard to tell the number of soldiers. They were in a long line from side to side. Some of their big horses shied away from one or more of the many, many prairie dog mounds. Suddenly, out of the blue wave of chargers, two riders bolted ahead and rode straight for the Hunkpapa lodges. Warriors forming in small bunches saw these two bold ones. One horse slightly ahead of the other, both soldiers broke over a rise and down into a shallow ravine, straight into a waiting group of warriors, breaking through their outer line. And then, in an instant, both were knocked from their horses. It was a sign that this day the great Hunkpapa medicine-man's vision would come to pass. The soldiers had fallen at the very edge of the Hunkpapa camp circle.

Gall ignored the growing noise of battle for a time as he carried his family one by one into the lodge. Bullets had ripped into them. Soldier bullets. Now and then, more soldier bullets whined over-head, some tearing through the lodge. The Hunkpapa warrior cast one last longing look at his loved ones. Then his eyes turned hard and black. He grabbed his repeating rifle and war club and swung onto his horse.

As he rode up with his shirt shredded in mourning, some warriors looked puzzled and cast questioning glances at one another. The Hunkpapa ignored them and went to Black Moon.

"What is happening with the soldiers?" he wanted to know.

Bullets whined over their heads. Some kicked up dust here and there. Warriors all around them were running their horses, working them up to their second wind. The two Hunkpapa war leaders sat their horses calmly and talked of what to do. Black Moon pointed to his right, toward the end of the soldier line closest to a low bluff.

"That seems to be the thinnest," he observed. "Fewer soldiers there."

Gall nodded. "Good. We will charge at them there."

Sitting Bull rode up, a knowing look passing through his eyes as he saw Gall's torn shirt.

"Uncle," Gall said. "It is good you are here. My cousin has seen a weak spot in the soldier line. On that end, toward that low rise. We should charge them there."

Sitting Bull agreed. "It is good."

"Uncle," Gall said. "It would be good if you would allow me to lead this charge. Besides, the warriors who are still coming need to be told what is happening."

The medicine-man nodded, almost imperceptibly. "It is time to send these soldiers to a far-off place," he said.

Gall spun his horse and rode among the milling warriors.

"Listen!" he shouted. "I will ride at the horse soldiers. They must be stopped. I welcome anyone who would join me!"

Without a backward glance, the Hunkpapa warrior turned his black horse toward the approaching soldiers and urged it into a lope. Warriors streamed behind him like a roaring, blurring flood.

As they neared the soldier line, many of the Lakota warriors saw that a few Arikara were riding with the bluecoats. Arikara. Old, old enemies of the Lakota. It was easy to understand now how the soldiers could find this camp. Lakota guns erupted, and the left flank of the approaching soldier line collapsed almost immediately. The Arikara turned their horses toward the river, to the cover of heavy timber along the Greasy Grass, and left their bluecoat friends to face the oncoming Lakota.

The soldier line halted. Some jumped from their horses and dropped to their knees to fire weapons. A few stayed on their horses and led bunches of other horses to the rear. Some disappeared into a thin stand of timber, trying to find good cover for the horses.

Gall turned the warriors back. Soldiers on foot and kneeling could take steadier aim. The Lakota must try something else.

Some of the more daring Lakota warriors continued to charge, alone or in twos and threes. This seemingly foolish tactic had a purpose. The soldiers were tricked into using their bullets without doing much damage, and some among them fell, one or two hit by arrows. More and more warriors charged in front of the soldier line, hidden by the dust and gun smoke. The soldier line wavered a little, and then they were regrouped. For a time they advanced, crawling toward the encampment through the prairie dog mounds and the low sagebrush. Groups of warriors swept at them through the haze of dust and smoke. Soldiers went down. Their advance stopped once more.

Warriors, perhaps two to three hundred, broke from the edge of the encampment in a two-pronged charge, Black Moon at the head of one, Gall at the other. The soldiers responded with a firing like one single roar, but soon the rapid firing slowed. Guns were beginning to jam. Dust billowed and swirled, kicked up by the flying hooves of Lakota war horses, making it difficult for the soldiers to take a good shot even when their guns were not jamming. And there was not one heartbeat of time unfilled with noise. Guns boomed. Bullets passed by with a high-pitched whine. They tore into chests and lungs with a hollow thud, and into arms and legs with a lighter crack. They hit the dust and ricocheted with a lower, longer whine. Here and there, a soldier would suddenly grunt and crumple to the dust. Some jerked their arms and legs as they died.

Now and then a warrior's horse screamed as a soldier's

bullet tore through its legs or chest, and pitched its rider headlong to the ground. Some who fell in such a way would scramble to their feet and move away from the firing. Some did not move, even as another warrior dashed in to retrieve them. The battle was now fully joined, and the soldier line began to waver.

The first shouts of alarm had startled two young warriors dozing lazily in the shade of their shelter. Bear, slender and quick, was the first to his feet. Soldiers! There was a moment of indecision for the two, but only a moment.

They grabbed their weapons and ran for the horses. Mounted, they stared at one another in wide-eyed wonder, not knowing what to say. White Feather Tail spoke first.

"Cousin," he said, "Take care of yourself," with Bear nodding as he said, "Yes, and you, too."

Someone shouted and a man waved them toward a few warriors gathering. The two young Sicangu rode to join the group.

Good Weasel, an Oglala rode up to the group. "They say the soldiers are charging the Hunkpapa camp," he told them.

"Most of the warriors are going there. But I think some of us should stay along the river. We should watch the crossings carefully. No telling where else the soldiers might come, and if some should come through here while we are at the other end, it would be bad for the women and children.

There was wisdom in Good Weasel's words. The warriors in the small group all knew that he had fought well at the Rosebud. So they listened to him.

"There is a crossing over there," the Oglala went on, pointing off to the east. "Medicine Tail Creek. It is dry, and a good place for soldiers to hide. Some should go there and wait — on this side."

Five warriors broke from the group. "I know that crossing," one of them said. "We will stand there."

Good Weasel looked around at the remaining handful, two of which were White Feather Tail and Bear. "I will ride along the river," he said. "I will be glad if you can come with me. If there is nothing going on, we can move on down further, follow the river toward the Hunkpapa camp." That was a good plan. They all agreed.

The warriors moved off behind Good Weasel, the Sicangu cousins riding together. "Look!" a warrior shouted, pointing toward the south. They all saw it. A dust cloud high above the trees, rising slowly into the sky. And then beneath it, the distant pop of gunfire. Horses were urged into a high lope as the group moved toward the river. Behind them was still much excitement.

The alarm was still being carried through the encampment. Warriors hurried toward the sound of the fighting. Women shouted for their children. Here and there an old woman sang a strongheart song. Old men moved through the confusion, trying to calm everyone. Now and then they shouted encouragement to passing warriors. "Take heart!" they would say. "Be strong! You are Lakota! Remember the helpless ones!"

Good Weasel and his followers moved rapidly. People were all along the river, mostly old warriors armed and ready for a fight. Perhaps hoping for one. Sounds of gunfire from the south were steady now. Two or three of the young warriors looked off in that direction. But Good Weasel kept them together, keeping them to their plan.

"Be patient," he advised. "We will all have our chance. It is as the Hunkpapa medicine-man said. Many soldiers will fall."

They came to a sharp bend in the river. It turned back to the northwest and curved mostly southward again. There they came upon two old men, both with snow-white hair, and both armed with bows and arrows. "Grandfathers," Good Weasel greeted. "How is it with you?"

"We are watching the ridges across the river," one of them replied. "We have not seen any soldiers. But, of course, our old eyes cannot see far."

Good Weasel glanced up at the ridges across the water. "I

also see nothing," he assured the two old warriors. "Watch your-selves," he called as he rode off with his small group.

The two old men watched Good Weasel and his group move on. "Cousin," Spotted Elk said to his companion, Uses Cane, "how many arrows do you have?"

Uses Cane looked at his quiver. "Eight," he reported.

"I have only four," said Spotted Elk.

"That is good," countered Uses Cane. "Four is the medicine number. And besides, it is a good day to die!"

On a rise just east of the Itazipacola camp, Good Weasel and his warriors saw a large group of charging Lakota ride swiftly out of sight into the dust below a low rise. From Good Weasel's position, the line of soldiers and horses were dark specks fading in and out of the dust. Then everyone in the group saw a small group of riders whipping their horses toward the cover of timber near the river. Behind the fleeing riders, the soldiers stopped their charge and began to fight on foot. A few soldiers still mounted were leading horses to cover in the trees close to the river. Good Weasel looked around. More and more warriors were coming from the upper camps. Soon his small band grew to over thirty. With this many warriors, he knew they could cause much trouble for the soldiers. He had an idea.

"Listen!" he called. "As you can see, the soldiers are on foot. Their charge has stopped. They came like a lance thrust toward the belly, looking for a soft spot. But now they are on foot. That is *their* soft spot. Now we can thrust a lance at *their* belly." He pointed to the trees where the horse-holders had taken the soldier mounts. "All their horses are in there. If we run them off, the soldiers can only waddle like ducks out of water."

"*Hokahe!* Let us go!" A shout came from within the group of warriors. Good Weasel turned his horse east toward the river. White Feather Tail and Bear followed close. They reached the river and plunged in. On the other side they galloped across a long, open area. Twice more they crossed the water and finally flanked the soldiers from the east. Another crossing brought them into the heavy timber along the south bank.

Good Weasel spoke softly. "We leave our horses here," he advised. "Some of you with bows should try to hit the soldier horses with arrows. Scare them. Chase them away."

The trees and brush along the river were thick. Many places to hide, for both warrior and soldier. Warriors slid from their mounts. Some stayed back to watch and hold the horses. The others moved off silently into the cover of brush and trees. Those with bows slid them from their cases and strung them, and tied the quivers to the front. Arrows just below the hand which drew the bow.

Sounds of gunfire came steadily now, from the southwest.

From the open away from the trees, Good Weasel's group could hear the soldiers shouting. A faint shout came from the edge of the encampment, and then a sound like softly rolling thunder. It could only be a mounted Lakota charge. Good Weasel, using hand signals, dispersed the warriors.

Somewhere from within the timber were sounds of nervous stomping, the squeak of leather, and the jingle of iron bits. White Feather Tail tapped his cousin on the shoulder and pointed between some branches to their right. Beyond the openings, between criss-crossing tree branches, were bluecoat horses. The steady gunfire made them jumpy. Horseholders were working hard to keep the animals quiet.

White Feather Tail pulled a handful of arrows from the quiver and moved to a crouching position. The bluecoat horses were a long stone throw from the two Sicangu. This was a time for the three-arrows game. White Feather Tail moved a little ways to align himself with an opening in the canopy of leaves and branches overhead.

He gauged the distance to the horses and angled the bow and pulled. One after another, five arrows hissed upward. By the time the first reached its high point, flipped and hurtled earthward, the fifth was also in the air. All five followed the same path. The Sicangu warrior smiled at his cousin and waited for the arrows to fall. He did not have long to wait. Because the horses were held in tight bunches, two of the arrows impaled horseflesh. The two wounded animals squealed and jerked away from the holders. Now the sky was filled with arrows as other Lakota warriors used the three-arrows game in a deadly manner.

Willow, gooseberry, and chokecherry shafts turned into a hissing, lethal rain. It was all the horseholders could do to keep frightened horses from bolting. Some of the soldiers began to fire wildly into the timber, not knowing exactly where the arrows came from. Good Weasel and some of the warriors with guns returned fire. Bullets whipped through the trees around White Feather Tail and Bear, slapping at leaves and snapping off small branches. White Feather Tail waited for a lull, then sent some more arrows into the sky. Soldiers in the trees shouted. Horses squealed in fright, or pain.

The fighting in the open, among the sage and prairie dog mounds, was just as bad for the soldiers. Firing from the edge of the encampment grew steadier and closer. War cries reverberated through the dust and smoke. And there was the constant sound like slow, rolling thunder. Mounted warriors. Lakota and Cheyenne. Pressing the soldiers hard with the tactic they knew best. The sweeping, slashing charge. Any who stood before such charges often found their fighting spirit melting away, before they died by bullet, arrow, lance, or war club. And when the enemy was foolish enough to attack such a strong encampment, his chances for dying beneath the hooves of Lakota and Cheyenne war horses were more than good.

Crazy Horse arrived just ahead of some Cheyenne. A shout erupted among the gathered warriors, blocking out the sound of the gunfire from dusty meadows for a few heartbeats. They saw the man who now rode among them. Gall, with Sitting Bull, rode up to the Oglala war leader. Other war leaders joined them, Big Road, the Oglala, and Black Moon, the Hunkpapa among them. Amid the noise, the small group of Lakota war leaders talked calmly among themselves. Crazy Horse broke from the group and rode among the warriors.

"We must see to it that these soldiers do not attack another Lakota or Cheyenne camp," he said. "But remember Rosebud Creek. It was not easy there, and it is not easy here. Do not waste your bullets, those of you who have guns. Make the soldiers fire and let them waste theirs."

The soldier thrust at the great encampment had been stopped and turned aside. In a sudden surge, the soldiers moved toward the cover of the timber. By now Good Weasel and his group were not the only warriors in the trees. Others had been moving steadily into the timber. And the warriors who had stopped and turned aside the soldier charge, now swept behind and to the flanks of the bluecoat retreat. Though hard-pressed, many soldiers made it into the cover of the trees. But that did not remove them from danger.

The trees were full of warriors. Some coming in close enough to strike a soldier with a war club or run one through with a lance. But the close-in fighting was not without its price for the Lakota and Cheyenne. Some warriors went down inside the soldier lines. Dust and smoke filled the timber. And then came a new threat for the soldiers. Warriors set fires, driving the bluecoats into a panic. Driving them east along the river bends, where more warriors waited.

East of the Itazipacola camp, near a sharp bend in the river, two old warriors sat among the willows. Fighting had been most intense to the south of their position. As far as they could hear. Uneven ground, the dust and smoke, and the distance, and the dimness in the eyes brought on by the weight of many, many winters, made it difficult to see. But the experience of many past battles and a warrior's instincts told the two old warriors that things were not going well for the bluecoats. The battle was moving toward the river where the soldiers were plainly seeking cover. A foolish move, in the opinion of the two old warriors. Foolish because many warriors had ridden past the two old men, pushing hard to flank the soldiers from the east. And now the soldiers were trying to hide in the very places where many warriors were already hidden. Truly, Sitting Bull's vision from the Sun Dance was coming to pass.

Uses Cane touched his companion lightly, and ever so briefly, on the arm. "I find that my eyes have grown much weaker since last winter," he said. "So perhaps you can look up to that far ridge." Uses Cane pointed east across the river to an area along the bluffs. "I thought I saw some men on horses there, just a little while ago. But I am not sure."

Spotted Elk shaded his eyes with both hands and searched the skyline on the other side of the river. There was nothing, at first. Then, something moving beyond the ridges. Dark shapes. Bouncing like rabbits. Then Spotted Elk realized what he was seeing. The heads and shoulders of soldiers riding in small bunches, side-by-side. Then they were gone. But a thin dust cloud moved slowly behind the ridges. Spotted Elk knew that such a dust cloud could only be made by horses. Horses ridden by bluecoats, or warriors. But warriors would be moving in the opposite direction, toward the fighting.

"I think there is something up there, Cousin," the old warrior told his companion. "I don't think your eyes are as weak as you think they are."

The two old warriors managed to get the attention of a small group of warriors passing by. "It would be good if you could find the leaders, and tell them my cousin and I have seen soldiers on the ridge, across the river. It is hard to be certain. Our eyes are old … but maybe someone should send a scout or two across the river to see."

The warriors studied the ridge for a few moments. Nothing was visible. No men on horses. But there was an unmistakable line of dust. One of the warriors spoke. "Old eyes are better than no eyes, Grandfather," he said to Spotted Elk. "And we could do well to listen to old warriors who have seen much. We will take the news, Grandfather. *Hokahe!*"

Bear pulled his cousin down behind a low sand bank along the river. Bullets hit the water behind them. Soldiers were firing in blind panic, perhaps knowing they were in a hopeless way. The brush-fires helping to push them along. There was not time for the soldiers to take a deep breath.

"You have only have your arrows left," Bear told his cousin.

"And how many bullets do you have?" asked White Feather Tail, ducking at the sound of a bullet's whine.

"Seven," was the reply.

A yelling came from within the timber. The reason for it was soon plain. Soldiers mounted their horses and galloped toward the east. A fast retreat. In the open areas away from the trees, the soldiers were quickly hemmed in by hard-riding warriors. Some warriors rode into the retreating lines to tear a soldier from his horse or fire at point-blank range. It was a long, hard, running fight. Troopers fell but others kept riding. No soldier turned aside to rescue any that had fallen. Each was trying to save himself.

Warriors swept in from the right flank of the soldiers, and more came out of the trees along the river. The soldiers were beaten. They could only hope to save themselves now. And the warriors were determined that these bluecoated enemies would pay a high price.

Some of the warriors who had been harassing the soldiers in the timber scrambled for their horses. Sensing a victory, they all wanted to be in on the end of it. Bear caught his horse. But White Feather Tail's buckskin was gone. "Go!" he yelled. "I'll find a horse and catch up!"

For the first time since shots were fired, the cousins were

separated. Bear galloped hard along the river.

Falling in with a line of warriors racing to cut off the soldier escape, he crossed the river with them at a sharp bend. He crossed back over alone when he thought the warriors had veered too far to the left, away from the running bluecoats. Coming through some trees, he burst out into the open, and saw three soldiers ahead of him. He lifted his rifle and fired, but missed. The soldier on the left turned sharply into the timber. Bear followed, the paint dodging trees and weaving his way through the timber, making it hard for the warrior to take steady aim. A game trail led the soldier to the river's edge, but he had to force his horse to jump from a bank as high as a man's head. They disappeared in a spray of white and came up struggling. Bear's paint, fresher than the lathered sorrel ridden by the soldier, flew off the cut bank.

They came up out of the water a horse-length behind the soldier. The bluecoat turned a startled young face toward the oncoming warrior. He brought a handgun around and up into the Sicangu's face. It misfired or was empty. The lunging paint closed the distance between the two horses. Without conscious thought, Bear jumped. His arms came around the wide-eyed soldier and the two men plunged into the waters of the Greasy Grass. The soldier slipped from the warrior's grasp. As Bear's moccasined feet touched the sandy river bottom, he pushed upward and out of the water. Somehow the rifle was still in his left hand. He swung the stock and felt the jarring impact of the weapon against the soldier's head. The soldier twisted backward into the current and came up feet-first. His arms fluttered a little. Then he floated away, face still in the water.

The Sicangu stood for a moment, staring after the body of the dead bluecoat, oblivious to the boom of gunfire and the victory shouts of the other warriors. He looked down at his hands, and only then did he realize that the stock of the old rifle had completely broken off. A bullet sliced into the water nearby with a curious, gurgling splash. He suddenly felt the weight of his wet leggings and began looking around for his horse. The paint was on the far bank. A gun. He must have a gun, he thought. He ran to catch the horse.

The throng of soldiers and warriors swept around a bend in the river and turned slightly toward the east. The soldiers could not know it, but they were headed for an old crossing at the river. Once there, they plunged their spent horses off uneven banks. And there, the warriors thinned out the soldiers even more. Someone among the soldiers tried to move them across in an orderly manner, but the firing from the Lakota was too heavy and fast. Soldiers and horses fell together.

There was barely a trail up the opposite bank, only a narrow cut wide enough for one horse. It caused soldiers and horses to jam like driftwood. Some Lakota rode into their midst with lances and war clubs, cutting down soldiers almost at will. Unhorsed soldiers and loose, riderless horses filled the crossing. Still, many bluecoats managed to crawl or ride up the bank on the east side of the Greasy Grass. Some were weaponless as they scrambled up the steep trails toward the top of the bluffs, desperate to make it to the top of the ridge.

High sharp notes pierced the air, far above the shouts, screams, and booming guns. War flutes. Messengers rode in among the warriors still fighting. More soldiers! Soldiers somewhere in the hills across the river, riding for the other end of the encampment! Crazy Horse and Gall sent out a word for a quick gathering of warriors.

The noise of battle at the river crossing began to thin out as warriors moved out to answer the call of the war leaders. "Some warriors must stay here to keep these soldiers on the hill," Gall said. "The rest can ride to the other end of the encampment. We cannot let those soldiers cross the river and ride into the camps. *Hokahe!*"

White Feather Tail could not find his horse, nor could he catch another mount. Bear was already gone. There was still fighting inside the timber. The soldiers were frantic, but were not giving up easily. The Sicangu spotted three or four behind a dead horse. Crouching behind a burned-out buffalo-berry shrub, the river to his left, he loosed a few arrows and ducked behind cover. He could not tell the effect of his arrows, but he did hear a scream of pain from the general direction of the three soldiers. A bullet whined over his head and at the same instant he heard a sickening pop as it hit flesh. From the corner of his eye he saw a mounted warrior grab at his side and fall into the water.

The fallen warrior came up out of the water gasping. Blood flowed from a hole in his left side. White Feather Tail dropped his bow, shed the bowcase and quiver of arrows, and ran into the water. Bullets whined close. Some hit the water close by. He caught the wounded warrior under the arm, went to one knee to let the man fall over his shoulder. With the still-struggling warrior over one shoulder, he ran back for the cover of the river bank. The current swirled around his legs, and the wounded man was heavy. Halfway to the bank, White Feather Tail lost his balance and went down.

"Stand up! Stand up!" A voice came from somewhere behind. A man on a horse, a fan of eagle feathers tied into his hair, reached down an arm. White Feather Tail grabbed the wounded man around the waist and held out his hand to the mounted warrior. A bullet cracked into the warrior's upper thigh just as he took White Feather Tail's hand. The man jerked at the impact and came off his horse. The Sicangu went back under the water, one wounded man below him and a second on top of him. He swallowed water and came up coughing.

A blurry glimpse of the river bank sent a surge of hope and determination through him. He grabbed the first wounded man by the arms and pulled him through the water and onto a small grassy spot on the bank. He ran back, fell, got up and ran again, splashing until he reached the other wounded man. Bullets splashed into the water all around him and whined past his head. The second wounded warrior struggled to stand and reached out as White Feather Tail reached him.

Then the man collapsed. It was a long, long way to the safety of the bank. The Sicangu expected a bullet to take him down. Lungs burning, arms and legs losing strength, he stumbled as he reached dry ground. He dragged the man onto the low, grassy area. The first man bled from a hole above his left hip bone. The second was hit just below the groin and bleeding heavily.

White Feather Tail untied his own belt, pulled the knife and sheath off, and wrapped it around the thigh wound. He didn't know if it would stop the bleeding. It was all he could think to do. With his knife, the Sicangu cut off a piece of the first man's breech-clout, folded it into a pad, and tied it in place over the wound with the man's belt.

Now he looked around. The firing in the timber was moving away. Hoofbeats, screams, and gunfire faded away to the east. The battle was moving away. White Feather Tail looked at his charges. The hip-wound was conscious. The other was not. He knew he couldn't leave them here. Someone in the camps could tend to them, if he could take them back there somehow. Loose riderless horses were all around. He would have to catch one or two.

Mrs. Wooden Leg, Sioux in Custer Battle.
Outdoor seated portrait of the wife of Wooden Leg,
a seventy-eight year old Native American Northern Cheyenne
woman, wearing a long cotton dress and braids. She was eighteen
and in camp at time of Battle of the Little Bighorn.
J. G. Masters, August 1936. Courtesy of the Denver Public Library.
Call Number X-33359

Custer's last battle, "Boots & Saddles,"
by Frederic Remington, 1892, photo of the painting,
With his typical mastery of "story," Remington shows the Cavalry soldiers
getting ready to battle the "hostile Indians" on June 25, 1876, at what would
become known as the Little Bighorn Battlefield located in the land
of the Crow Nation in Montana. Date: 1892.
Courtesy of the Denver Public Library.
Call Number: X-33632.

CHAPTER 15

...uster: Feeling Free as the Golden Eagle

At last he felt unfettered, free as the golden eagle soaring majestically over the valley in search of prey.

The tiredness went away, along with any doubts where he stood with his legs spread apart in a poise of arrogant defiance, gazing with the scouts at a map they'd drawn in the dusty ground.

The map showed the lay of it all the way from the upper forks of Ash Creek to the bluffs guarding the Little Big Horn. He wanted no mistakes. Custer spoke as a commander to Smith, Yates, Keogh, Calhoun, and the scout, Bouyer. Back of them the troopers were tending to their horses, exchanging viewpoints, worries. The sun was almost overhead, baking down at them and the north for of Ash Creek.

Custer gestured. "What we have here is a series of bluffs pushing along the river. What you said, Bouyer, yes, these ridges further to the north lay like the backbones of ancient mares." The creative side of the Boy General filed all that away for future reference.

He nudged a dusty, black boot toe at the map, then went on,

141

"Here, there's an old lodgepole trail going down Medicine Tail Coulee. That's where we'll hit them."

Bouyer grunted an affirmation, but he was worried.

Custer continued, "Reno — should be down at the river by now."

The men looked at Custer, and at the map drawn in the ground, hoping that Custer's luck would hold out and that they wouldn't later be falling dead and defeated to the lonely ground.

To Keogh he said, "Further than we have to go. He'll water the horses, detail his battle plan. What we don't want is to attack first. Timing, wins battles." A smile for everyone. "Well, let's not keep the Sioux waiting."

The rest stop consumed well onto ten minutes by Adjutant Cooke's watch. As they moved out, he hung in close to Custer, then the color bearers. Now the route taken by Custer brought them up a shallow ravine toward the rougher heights set back from the river. No longer could they see Reno's battalion. There'd been a few questions as to what Benteen had encountered. And it was expected that Benteen's three companies would support Reno.

Angling to the northwest on this windless day, it was Custer halting the column when Curly and the handful of scouts came over to a rise, to tell Custer the floodplain was full of lodges. Then on again, at a brisker pace, Custer's face gaunt and wind-burnt, the chestnut sorrel Vic just as saddlesore and weary. Behind Custer, who seemed unaware of it, a lot of horses were beginning to lag. Sweat stained the soiled clothing of the men. Their fear was of being left behind — and they knew Custer's wrath if this happened.

But how much longer would their sweaty and lathering horses respond to the bloody spur rakings across their trembling flanks? The pace continued, at a gallop, until there came the gradual, far-off rattle of gunfire. Coming to a low spot giving them a glimpse of the floodplain clogged with pillars of dust, Custer rose in his stirrups and yelled, "See, there they are! Reno and his boys are beginning to attack!"

Around Custer there came excited cheering; and with some troopers unable to control their horses lunging ahead of their commander. "Steady'em down, boys," yelled Custer jubilantly. "There are enough Indians to go around."

Again George Armstrong Custer urged his gelding into a gallop, keeping behind the higher ridges to avoid being seen by his enemies. More and more horses simply quit their riders, drawing back, and further back, and even the scouts were having a hard time with their ponies.

Back leading his C Company, Captain Tom Custer was among the first to notice a horse soldier galloping in from the south, then another officer called out that it was one of Reno's men, Trooper McIlhargy. As a call came down to halt the column, Tom Custer beckoned to Sergeant Kanipe.

"Sergeant, go find Captain McDougall. Tell McDougall to bring his pack-train straight to us. If any packs come loose, cut them and come on. Go quickly! Tell McDougall there's a big Indian village ahead. If you see Captain Benteen, tell him to hurry up." The urgency, he felt, justified his actions, that they'd be facing a superior force.

Captain Tom Custer said again, "A big Indian village ..."

Up with the scouts clustered nearby, George Custer interpreted Trooper McIlhargy's message to mean that the Sioux were breaking camp and trying to make a go for the Big Horn Mountains. Impatient for a head-on collision with the enemy, he led his command over a ridge and swung to the north behind some bluffs. Though louder, the firing was from the west was more erratic, which only served to have Custer pick up a faster gallop, with wider gaps between the companies.

When Custer brought his command to another halt, it was with a hard abruptness. Alone he broke for a scouting excursion to the top of a bluff. In closer now, he picked out over a hundred lodges, the dust and smoke and other bluffs hiding the larger part of the encampment. From here he took in Reno's battalion engaging the Sioux. Quickly he wheeled Vic around, to angle toward his waiting Regiment, and to wave them onward. Out here he knew just how deceptive distances can be, but Custer knew he'd been right when viewing this valley from up at Crow's Nest — close to eight miles from back there to the bluffs he was approaching.

The firing, he realized was much louder, as he could pick out the individual sounds of the new Springfields over the Henrys, Winchesters, Ballards, the weaponry of the Sioux.

Adding to this was the crackling of the fire consuming brush along the river, as viewed by Custer when he brought his Regiment toward the last high bluff to have the floodplain reveal what it held. This time, going with Custer were Adjutant Cooke, Captain Tom Custer, Autie Reed, and Trumpeteer John Martin.

Where before Reno's battalion had been out of the floodplain, now Custer realized a battle was being waged in timberland next to the river. All he could see among the many lodges of the Sioux were a few ponies, and some women and children and dogs, and he exulted, "We've caught them sleeping!"

"I wouldn't be so sure, General," cautioned Lieutenant Cooke.

Custer turned to Captain Tom Custer. "You sent someone to hurry up the pack train …?"

"At your orders, Autie," replied Tom.

"Just to make sure, send someone else," the Boy General said.

Captain Tom Custer nodded to Lieutenant Cooke and said, "Send Martin."

The adjutant motioned to Trumpeteer Martin, who drew closer. Cooke started to give him verbal instructions, when he stopped to pull out a notebook, to lay it against his knee. Martin, an Italian immigrant, had a limited vocabulary, and Cooke, as he scribbled out a message to bring up the packs, wanted to be absolutely certain there were no misunderstandings.

"Here, take this to Captain Benteen …"

The note buttoned in his pocket, Giovanni Martini, now Trumpeteer John Martin, as he was known to the men of the 7th, started off the upper reaches of the bluff and in the same direction taken by Sergeant Kanipe sometime ago. He passed the Crow scouts and Mitch Bouyer, who were huddled apart from the Regiment.

The words of the Boy General had carried through the nooning of this day to Bouyer. Is Yellow Hair still blinded by his lust for a victory over the Sioux? For even Bouyer could see some movement in the encampment, and over the firefight taking place along the river, he could hear the drumbeat of thousands upon thousands of Indian horses surging around on the floodplain beyond the lodges. As for Yellow Hair not seeing any warriors, they too numbered in the thousands.

"He is blind," Bouyer uttered silently as the order came to proceed along the edge of the bluffs.

This brief rest interlude had given those lagging behind barely enough time to rejoin their companies. But there was a new eagerness on the faces of the horse soldiers seeing the encampment for the first time. Even the horses sensed this mood change, and still, as the Regiment went cantering over a hill rolling gently toward the brushy mouth of Medicine Tail Coulee, a few horses stumbled or went to their knees out of sheer exhaustion. Curses became the order of the day.

Besides Curly, there were three other Crow scouts: Goes Ahead, White Man Runs Him, and Hairy Moccasin. They could discern warriors slipping through the smoke and dusty haze gripping the encampment, and they lagged behind even more.

Coming to a high point, Harry Moccasin, reining up, was echoed by the others and by Mitch Bouyer.

Just ahead the Regiment commanded by Captain Yellow Hair was cantering over a hill all in bloom, loco weed painted a variety of colors: rose, white, pink and lavender, magenta and deep purple, flowers that were being crushed into the loamy soil by shod hooves.

To the Crow this was the sacred hill of the wild peas. For their women would come to pluck buffalo beans from the flowers and boil them in meat kettles. First the Sioux had come trampling here, now the horse soldiers. Hairy Moccasin remembered, as he'd been part of it, this was the hill where the youths went for their puberty dreams.

And along with Hairy Moccasin all of the Crow knew that Custer was destined to come here, as surely as the Iron Horse cannot leave its trails of iron. There was a stirring to his left. It was the half-blood, Bouyer, directing his words at Curly.

"You are very young," intoned the half-blood. "This is no place for you to die. Go to those other soldiers, there at Yellowstone. Tell them all of us here are killed."

The half-blood spurred on toward the Regiment just passing into the upper moth of Medicine Tail Coulee.

For a while Curly held there, watching the horse soldiers go deeper into the coulee, unaware that the other Crow scouts had left to head easterly across the valley of the Little Big Horn.

While at the head of his command, George Armstrong Custer found it to be harder going in the downsloping coulee. But since it was the only way at this point along the river to gain entrance to the Sioux encampment, he had no other choice than to ride on. The Coulee walls were sheer and narrow, the ground a hard pebbly loam carpeted with a thin layer of prairie grass, and thorny thickets and willows lashed out at passing horsemen.

In close to Custer were Cooke and Tom Custer and the Regimental first-sergeant, the forked-tail flags held by the bearers drooping limply as the air was eerily calm. A smile from Custer at what happened back in Rosebud, at night when they'd made camp, his personal standard falling backwards twice — an omen of bad luck, some officers had proclaimed.

"Custer's luck," he said in gazing off at his brother, Tom. "How are they faring back there?"

"Cursing their way down, Autie. Which means they'll take their anger out on the Sioux. But still trying to hold in a column of twos. We'll probably have to cross the river that way. Or unless, Autie, you've got orders to the contrary?"

"Gentlemen," said Custer, upon realizing the coulee was opening up now to reveal a low level stretch of land passing toward the riverbank less than fifty yards away, "My only order is — att … attack!" In his growing excitement the Boy General stuttered. He also took note of higher bluffs to the north, the firefight and hellous smoke and dust opposite. "Once we're in the village we'll hit right to support Reno. But, most assuredly, attack!"

From nearby came sporadic rifle-fire, with Adjutant Cooke calling out that some Indians were firing at the Regiment.

This barely registered to Custer, bursting out of the coulee, revolver in hand, pushing on over a grassy, roundish amphitheater of level land. He realized now that he was at the extreme northern end of the encampment pushing in close to the river, judged quickly that here the river banks were high and it would be difficult crossing.

But he would not be denied now, his Glory!

Custer's last battle, "Unhorsed,"
courtesy of the Denver Public Library,
by Frederic Remington, magazine illustration from January, 1892,
Call Number: X-33634.
This depicts one of Custer's Seventh Cavalrymen on the ground
with his gun in hand immediately after he has been unhorsed,
while a Sioux warrior on horseback aims at the soldier with his rifle.
Remington captures the moment perfectly.

CHAPTER 16

Walks Alone: Defending the Camp

It pleased Walks Alone to know that he could stay behind to help defend the camp if any soldiers came. And his new father told him of the news brought by scouts. Soldiers were in the north country, near the Yellowstone.

"Soldiers are all around," Good Owl said. "Since my grand-father's time, they have been here, wanting to push us off our lands. That is why we must always be prepared to defend ourselves." Good Owl gazed softly at his new son, inwardly pleased that the boy liked the gift of the old rifle. The boy would be a strong warrior before too many winters passed. "Do you understand what I have said?"

Walks Alone nodded, and grasped his rifle tighter.

The sun was in the middle of the sky as Walks Alone wandered near the river, far to the south of Medicine Tail Creek. He watched some women and children digging for *tinpsila*, the turnips. A few of the children played in the water.

From somewhere to the south came a sudden commotion.

Horses running. People shouting. Soldiers!

The word spread quickly. The women and children! Protect them! Walks Alone had been watching people quickly scattering back toward the camps. He stayed, sitting low in a clump of buffalo grass, clutching the rifle.

Then it came, from the south end of the encampment. Gunfire. Walks Alone looked toward the sound, anxious eyes trying to probe the dense green foliage. He caught flashes of painted warriors swooping on their war horses toward the rattling gunfire. Gunfire which came faster, and closer.

It would have been easy to run and find a place to hide. But Walks Alone felt an urge to stay. To fight. Between restless bouts of sleep last night had come the words of Eagle That Talks. Of his dream. What did he, a boy, have to do with the great medicine-man's vision? What did the Oglala's dream mean? For fear of being misunderstood, he had not told his new father about the old warrior's dream.

More and more warriors rode toward gunfire. Walks Alone rose to stare up at the bluffs fronting the other side of the river. Around him swirled cottony seeds. Sent by spirits, according to Eagle That Talks.

"I must find him," Walks Alone whispered fiercely. There was no wind along the river to send sandy dust gritting across the meadows. Still, there was in the air the brittle feel of dust and a strange anticipation. He wanted to find the old Oglala. His friend.

Moving in closer to the river, he started north, though, at times, he would cast a glance bluffward as visions of soldiers falling into camp hurried his steps. With the agility of youth, he broke into a run for the northern reaches of the camps.

Veering away from the river, Walks Alone ran with both hands wrapped around his precious rifle. He saw women and children hurrying out of the camps, moving west toward the safety of the low hills. The frenzy of activity all around sent dust clouds swirling upward, thick and choking. Warriors rode through the camps, shouting war cries and moving toward the gunfire.

Walks Alone narrowly avoided a mounted warrior as he ran among a group of brush shelters on the northern edge of the camps. He turned aside and ran among the lodges of the Oglala camp, to the lodge of Eagle That Talks. He crouched in through the open door flap to find the lodge empty. Back outside, he saw several old men standing together, taking in the sounds of battle to the south. He darted over to an Insanti, an old man whose dark face seemed to be all furrows and ridges, but whose eyes sparkled.

"Have you seen the Oglala, Eagle That Talks?"

"Grandson, these old eyes see little anymore."

"But I must find him!"

"Then look down by the big crossing. Medicine Tail Creek."

Walks Alone whirled toward the river, sprinting across the open spaces until he saw a small cluster of old men. A smile etched his face when he picked out the Oglala. But why was everyone staring across the river, he wondered.

He followed the direction of their gaze, and saw the horse soldiers. They were coming down the dry cut of Medicine Tail Creek!

Walks Alone broke into a desperate run, his blood going cold. His only thought was to get there to protect Eagle That Talks. It was not that far to where the old ones stood. A weak arrow's cast. But it seemed an unreachable distance to a twelve year old boy. The rifle was an added burden.

His frenzied yell brought a few glances away from the river. The old ones were hugging in close to sheltering willows and scattered clumps of brush. Then they turned back to a more pressing sight — horse soldiers just about to burst out of the dry bed of Medicine Tail Creek.

Five Lakota warriors who had been close to the river moved back a little. Five Cheyennes came riding in from their camp. The warriors and old men, for the time being, were the only defense

151

against the approaching soldiers. Fifteen against so many soldiers.

Walks Alone remembered he was carrying an empty rifle. He stopped and fumbled a shell out of the doeskin pouch. He worked the lever that opened the slot in the side of the rifle, fumbled in the shell, then jacked it into the breech. Then he ran toward a nearby cottonwood.

He steadied the rifle against the tree. The barrel wavered, as the pure fear and excitement of the moment shined in Walks Alone's eyes. The first column of soldiers came out of the dry creek bed and onto a level place. Fork-tailed banners waved above them. In the lead was a soldier in buckskins riding a tall sorrel horse.

The boy felt as if his lungs would burst as he sighted in on the soldier in buckskins. He steadied, and squeezed the trigger. Even as the rifle's kick drove him back, he saw the soldier in buckskins twist in the saddle and begin to fall. Other soldiers came quickly to the falling man, to keep him on his sorrel horse.

The warriors and old men kept up their firing, even as the soldiers returned fire. One of the old men went down. At the water's edge, the horse soldiers milled around, like ducks in a hailstorm.

A bullet plunked into the tree just above the boy's head, bringing the realization of danger. A gnarled hand pulled at Walks Alone's shoulder.

"Keep down ... behind the tree," hissed the Oglala, Eagle That Talks. They both crouched behind the shelter of the tree.

Together they watched the soldiers scramble away to the north and up another arm of Medicine Tail Creek. Together they watched as many Lakota warriors reached the crossing and rode across in pursuit of the fleeing soldiers.

Together, they knew they were seeing the power of a great vision.

BATTLE OF THE BIG HORN.

Battle of the Big Horn
Illustration of how the media portrayed Custer
at the Battle of the Greasy Grass (the Little Bighorn).
Kurz and Allison. October 15, 1889.
Courtesy of the Library of Congress.

A drawing by Chief Red Horse, a participant in the battle,
providing an eyewitness account of what happened
at the Battle of the Greasy Grass (the Little Bighorn) on June 25, 1876.
Courtesy of the Smithsonian Institution.

CHAPTER 17

Like Leaves Scattered by a Whirlwind

Word had quickly filtered back into camp that the attacking soldiers had been beaten back. It was carried by warriors returning for fresh horses. The people still in the camps, mostly the old ones, took the news with smiles of relief. A few old men lifted a thin war cry. Some old women trilled for the victory and hastened to prepare for the returning warriors, knowing that some might be hurt. Or dead. Messengers were sent west and north, to the women, children, and old people who had fled to hide and wait out the fighting. The encampment began to breathe a sigh of relief when word came about more soldiers, this time coming from the hills across the river. Relief and exhilaration, just beginning to build, was snuffed out like a flame smothered by a heavy, wet blanket. There was nothing to do but meet this new threat.

A Cheyenne warrior, one of only a handful left in his camp, saw the soldiers on the hill. They had reined to a halt, sitting their horses in groups of four-across. Then, to the warrior's dismay, the soldiers started down a cut that gradually widened as it went down toward the river. Pejuta Sinte Wakpa, the Lakota called it — Medicine Tail Creek. And the soldiers were coming fast.

The warrior, Bobtail Horse, wondered for a moment if the Lakota and Cheyenne fighting on the south end of the encampment could be alerted in time to prevent the soldiers from riding into camp. No, he decided. The soldiers were already getting close to the river. But something had to be done. Someone had to try. Bobtail Horse began to raise the alarm. The Cheyenne lodges would certainly be in danger if the soldiers came across the river. Two warriors who had been riding guard just outside the camp circle came galloping in.

Bobtail Horse pointed toward Medicine Tail Creek. "We must fight!" he yelled. "Gather everyone you can! Those soldiers must not be allowed to cross the river! Even if it is the last thing we do."

Five rode out of the Cheyenne camp toward Medicine Tail Creek. Soldiers, more than could be counted, filled the steep-sided ravine, a long, gray-blue avalanche sliding toward the water. Five against so many. Unimaginable odds. Yet, there was no other choice.

Bobtail Horse and his warriors raced toward the point at which the soldiers would have to ford the river. They were briefly joyous at the sight of a handful of Lakota already in the area opposite the crossing. Some with rifles. Bobtail Horse and his Cheyennes rode in line, side by side. Two of the warriors began to sing their death songs.

The point of the soldier line was already at the bottom, and they filed the ravine all the way back to the top. Then, strangely, they stopped. On the camp side of the crossing the Cheyenne and Lakota spread themselves out along the river, finding whatever cover was available. They fired their guns and shouted, trying to make the soldiers think there were more then the ten or fifteen waiting for them. A soldier's shout came across the river and the first small group of them urged their big horse into the river.

Bobtail Horse began to sing his death song. For a few heartbeats the Lakota and Cheyenne guns were silent, and the slashing made by the big bluecoat horses in the water could be plainly heard. Then, the warrior guns erupted in one single volley, and arrows hissed across the water.

The battle along Greasy Grass had taken a new turn.

Crazy Horse and Gall were quick to send warriors toward the upper camp to meet the new threat. But it was a long hard gallop through the camp or along the river. Some warriors veered toward ponies for fresh mounts. Others raced for their lodges, hoping that the horses left picketed were still there. Crazy Horse urged his mare toward the Oglala camp as fast as she could go. But she was spent. The camps were not completely deserted, but they were in disarray. Some lodges had been taken down. Here and there only a set of poles stood, the lodgeskin having been taken off. Personal belongings and household articles were everywhere, dropped or left by the fleeing women and children. Some wounded and dead warriors had already been brought back into the camps. Families tended the injured, or gathered to grieve for the lost ones.

The Oglala warrior reached his own lodge to find Black Shawl standing with the jaw rope of the buckskin gelding. He quickly told her of the fight at the other end of the camp, and of Gall's tragedy. Then he asked her to go to the safety of the low hills to the west. She declined.

"The wife of the greatest warrior in the valley should not run to hide," she told him. She took the jaw rope of the worn-out mare and handed him the rope for the buckskin. And a bag of bullets he had forgotten earlier. He held her gaze for a long moment. There was no fear in her dark eyes. Only determination. Truly, such a woman was worth a warrior's death.

Gunfire came from the east, across the river. The Oglala warrior swung onto the buckskin and rode through his camp circle, calling for warriors. Then to the Sicangu camp. The sound of the increasing gunfire told him that the warriors who had been fighting the first attack had reached the upper end of the encampment. The gunfire was moving away, it seemed. The Oglala and Sicangu responded to his call and gathered strong around him. Many on fresh horses. Some with new soldier rifles. He looked up into the sky. The sun was nearly to the halfway point on the downward slide to the west. It was hot and a few clouds could be seen. A beautiful day. A good day to die … for the soldiers.

Crazy Horse led the Oglala and Sicangu camps. He wanted to prevent the soldiers from finding another way to invade the camps, or cut off their escape if they were running. More and more warriors joined as the entire throng broke into a gallop. The Oglala leader twisted to look back. And he, the glorious warrior who had led many warriors into many battles, was awed by the sight. There were fully three, maybe four hundred warriors riding behind him. There was no crossing at the spot where they went into the water. They made one. It was as if the water boiled as the warriors moved across. Then a sound like a low thunder rolled up the opposite slope. The Oglala and Sicangu were riding strong. Shadowy, undulating shapes inside the dust cloud raised by hundreds of pony hooves. Surely, a sight to weaken the heart of the strongest enemy.

As Crazy Horse was calling for warriors in the Oglala and Sicangu camps, Gall, the Hunkpapa still in his torn shirt, was leading a large group of Hunkpapa, Miniconju, and Itazipacola warriors across the ford at the bottom of Medicine Tail Creek. Crow King, another Hunkpapa war leader, had crossed shortly before. Crow King's group had been hard on the heels of the soldiers who had retreated up the north cut of Medicine Tail Creek. The soldiers had advanced only to the middle of the river before they turned back. Stopped, somehow, by the brave little group of Cheyenne and Lakota.

The soldiers had fallen back to the safety of the steep-walled cut of Medicine Tail Creek, taking their wounded with them. They had dismounted, and then were forced to scramble up out of the dry cut as the first group of warriors responding to this new threat arrived at the ford. Leading their horses, the soldiers climbed out of both forks of the coulee. They ran until they gained a sharp rise. Some were cut down along the way.

A group of Cheyenne with a small number of Lakota crossed the river at nearly the same spot Crazy Horse had earlier. As this group came up out of the gullies from the river, they saw the soldiers pinned down on the rise. Without hesitation, they charged. But the bluecoats responded with heavy fire. Warriors went down, one of the Cheyenne leaders among the first to die. The Cheyenne circled back and gathered for another charge. This time, though, the soldiers stood their ground and again poured heavy fire into the charging warriors. More of the soldiers fell. The firing was continuous now, from both sides. The fire from the hard-charging warriors took a toll in both horses and bluecoats. Dead horses were an ominous trail, leading from where the soldiers broke out of the cut to their position on the rise. Wounded and frightened horses pulled away from their holders and ran in panicked flight. But there was a trail of dead bluecoats, too.

East of this beleaguered group, in the area between the two forks of Medicine Trail Creek, another group of soldiers was trying to make its way to the northwest. Both soldier groups had their eyes and their hopes on a hill to the northwest of Medicine Tail Creek. Trying the age-old, classic military maneuver of gaining the high ground. But this day the soldiers were paying a fearful price for every step toward that hill. And with each fallen soldier, hope was diminished. For it seemed that warriors were rising out of the Earth itself.

By now, it was plain to the Lakota and Cheyenne. This second soldier thrust at the encampment had failed. Now the soldiers were the defenders. The Lakota and Cheyenne were pressing the attack.

Dust billowed. It rose, swirled, and then hung heavily in the air, a gray death shroud over the hills and gullies just northeast of the Greasy Grass River. Warriors moved in and out of the grayness. Blurred, barely discernible shapes, suddenly appearing in a soldier's field of vision, then disappearing. Then another. And another. And then a group of dark, blurry shapes flashing out of the dust, or over a rise, flying at the soldiers like a horde of angry hornets with a deadly sting. Stinging the intruder, then swooping away.

And with every few heartbeats, another soldier fell.

Sounds of battle carried clearly into the sprawling encampment. There was almost as much activity in the camps as there was on the gullies and ridges just beyond the Greasy Grass. Some of those who had fled to the west and north were returning, relieved to know that the enemy was not in the camps. Dead and wounded warriors were carried back to their lodges. Medicine men and women were busy, helping where they could. But it was mostly families who tended to their wounded, or sadly accepted the bodies of their fallen warriors.

Movement to and from the horse herds was constant. A few loose horses moved through the maze of people, lodges, trees, and camp paraphernalia. Some had plainly broken from the herds, and some were refugees from the fighting at the south end of the encampment, painted for war and dragging long jaw-ropes. Riderless.

A man with a strong face rode through the camp circles. Before one lodge he spoke gently to a wounded warrior. At another he shared the grief of a family which had just learned of the death of their warrior. And to a passing group of warriors he would cry, "Be strong! Harden your hearts toward the enemy who comes! There are many helpless ones here." Sitting Bull kept moving. Encouraging the warriors. Reassuring the women, children, and old ones. "Our warriors are strong today," he told them. "The soldiers will not come into the camp. This day is ours!"

Inside the lodge in the Oglala camp, a young warrior heard the words of the Hunkpapa holy man as he finished painting his face. He glanced over at the old woman who sat holding his weapons and shield in her lap. Her face, lined with the deep furrows and the wisdom of time, could not help but let a little pride show through. But there was worry behind the pride. His wound from the fight on the Rosebud, with Three Stars, had not completely healed.

"Grandmother," he said tenderly, "I was just a boy when my father was killed in the fight with the soldiers beyond Lodgepole Ridge. In my grief I was angry, but you drove away the anger with something you said. I remember those words. Do you remember what you said to me?"

The old woman smiled, dark eyes shining. Behind them she briefly caressed the memory of a strong, quiet, son. Young Black Wolf's father. Then she spoke the words to her grandson again. "It is better to lie like a warrior in death," she said, "than to be wrapped up well with a heart of water inside."

Black Wolf smiled and stood. "I will remember those words until I die," he told her. "But today is not my day to die. I will fight the soldiers, and I will return." He paused at the door, eyes twinkling. "And I will be hungry for some good turnip soup."

The young warrior took the jaw-rope of the sturdy little gray from his mother and lightly touched her face, drawing a smile from her worried features. He tucked one end of the long rope under the belt and swung onto the gray. From his grandmother he took the weapons and shield. "Turnip soup," he said, and rode away toward the sounds of the battle.

A man, in a shirt hanging in tattered remnants, led a force of mounted warriors up out of a gully near the head of the north fork of Medicine Tail Creek. They were greeted by a thin volley from the retreating soldiers moving toward a low rise. Gall quickly looked to the southeast, not wanting his warriors to be hit from behind, looking for rifles and ammunition. Crow King's warriors, Gall surmised. They had ridden up the north fork of the creek ahead of him.

The Hunkpapa leader quickly organized a charge toward the soldier ranks, urging those warriors with firearms to take the point. Return fire from the soldiers was heavy, once they stopped to form a line. A few warriors went down, some dragged away from the firing by their running horses. Others were quickly rescued by another warrior dashing into the rain of soldier bullets. Gall turned back his warriors. He knew in his heart that these soldiers would be driven away and defeated. It would not be necessary to take foolish risks to do so. Clearly, this day the Lakota were strong. Foolishness was not a mark of strength. Or wisdom. He called the warriors together.

"Those of you with guns should move at the soldiers on foot. Stay low, hide yourselves, and wait for a good shot. Those of you with bows, find good hiding places and send up arrows to fall on the soldiers and their horses."

Crazy Horse came up on a small flat in time to see a small group of soldiers turn and spur their mounts back toward the main group, toward the east. He quickly sent a scouting party toward the north. From the sound of the firing to the east, there were many soldiers. But there could be others hiding in the gullies and behind the ridges all around.

He moved his large group toward the firing at a gallop. Up over a rise they could finally see groups of soldiers. Most were dismounted, firing as they ran or dropping to a knee to take careful aim. One group of mounted soldiers moving southward down a long slope turned aside to meet them. The soldiers' guns boomed and bullets whistled in among the warriors. Crazy Horse's Oglala and Sicangu warriors quickly returned fire, but it was another group of warriors who turned the soldiers back to the north. A number of Cheyenne and Lakota warriors came up out of the ravine to Crazy Horse's right. Some were mounted but many were on foot. They poured heavy fire into the soldiers' left flank, forcing them to retrace their path back up the slope.

Warriors all around the Oglala war leader broke off alone or in small groups, eager to get in the fight. Many rode at the soldiers, some going down from the heavy fire. From his position, Crazy Horse could see that the soldiers were being pushed or were moving toward a ridge. There was not much cover on that ridge, but it was a high point. If the soldiers reached it and formed themselves into several firing lines, too many good Lakota and Cheyenne could be lost trying to dislodge them. The Oglala passed the word to his right and left. He would lead a charge.

Once again, hundreds of hooves made the noise of slow rolling thunder. At the point of a high, billowing dust cloud, the Oglala and Sicangu warriors swooped toward the groups of soldiers. Some of the bluecoats held steady and fired. Many ran up the slope. The point of the charge turned right, forming a long, sweeping curve of horsemen. That maneuver gave the warriors riding on the left a wide field of fire. And warrior guns boomed. Many soldiers fell. Many, many soldiers.

The line of mounted warriors stretched out as the charge slowed its momentum. Those with bullets to spare kept up a relentless fire as the soldiers scrambled for the ridge. Near the mouth of a ravine the warriors turned left and advanced up the slopes. Firing from the soldiers had noticeably thinned.

Crazy Horse rode back up the slope looking for a good vantage point, and to await the return of the scouting party he had sent north. On a slight rise he reined in the buckskin and looked to the east. Dust billowed upward from the areas of soldier or warrior movements. There was still gunfire. It seemed to the Oglala war leader that all of the warriors he could see, mounted or on foot, were moving east or north. Some late arrivals were coming up from the river. He guessed that the soldiers, or at least the largest group of them, were in one spot. A high ridge. East and up the slopes from his position. Gunfire came from other spots, too. From ridges and gullies to the southeast. And from the area near the mouth of Medicine Tail Creek.

He decided to move to a higher location. A handful of warriors rode with him and along the way the scouting party found him. They had pushed their horses on several hard sprints up and down the hills to the north, and proved the washes and gullies, they said. They saw no soldiers to the north.

Crazy Horse and his small following stopped at a rise west of the soldier position on the high ground. From there they could see that the bluecoats were formed into two or three lines, fighting on foot. Only a few mounted soldiers were moving through the dust and smoke behind those on the ground.

A few soldiers were still trying to join the force on the high ground. Most did not make it. Warrior sharpshooters brought them down. Or, here and there, a daring, hard-riding warrior sent a soldier sprawling into the dust with a swing of a war club. And now and then small bunches of warriors rode at the soldier lines on the high ground. Some went down, but many rode close enough to bring down a soldier with a few hurried shots before veering off.

Many warriors were fighting on foot now. Some worked their way behind cover toward the bluecoats on the hill. Some probed the draws and washouts, now and then dislodging a hiding soldier. Sometimes a group of them.

Black Wolf, the young Oglala, joined a group of about twelve warriors who had managed to trap some soldiers in a deep washout. Another group of warriors were creeping through the grass on the other side of the deep cut. With hand signals, the two groups spread themselves out all along the lip of the deep gully. At a signal, they would rush up to the edge and fire down into the bunched-up soldiers. Black Wolf saw that many of the warriors poised to attack had guns. Mostly newly acquired rifles, picked up during the fighting. Two or three had revolvers. The young Oglala was one of the three warriors with only a bow. An older warrior with two fresh scalps hanging from his belt raised his hand, glancing about to see that everyone was ready. Quick sporadic fire erupted beyond the rises to the northeast. Some of the warriors around the ravine flinched, nearly jumping up to fire prematurely. The man with the scalps swung his arm down and was the first to leap to the edge of the cut.

Nearly two dozen warriors were at the ravine's edge in less than a heartbeat, and the first combined volley down into the cut was one loud blast. Fresh rounds were chambered into rifle breeches, revolvers were cocked, and the sound of another volley tore the air. Acrid smoke hung above the ravine. There was no return-fire from the soldiers, only screams of anguish and pain.

"*Hiyupo!*" Someone spoke the command. "Come on!" And slid down the loose walls of the ravine. It was the warrior with the fresh scalps.

Black Wolf loosed an arrow at a soldier slowly raising a rifle, then jumped into the ravine. The arrow took the soldier in the throat, pinning him to the dirt. Only a handful of soldiers were still alive. They were quickly dispatched with the swing of a war club, or the slash of a knife. The hot little fight in the ravine was over. Warriors scrambled back up and out with fresh scalps and turned their attention to the gunfire further up the slopes.

With their new guns, they were determined to kill more soldiers. Sitting Bull's vision was coming to pass. Today the Lakota were very strong, fighting like the wolf to protect their homes and families.

Young Black Wolf stopped to rest behind a small knoll. He wanted to look at his new weapon. It was heavy. The small black case on the belt held more bullets than he could hold in one palm. He had seen Good Weasel load one of these things, and Black Wolf had a good memory for such things. Soon, he had a round chambered. He rested a moment or two more before he started up the slope. His wounded side was throbbing.

Gall, the Hunkpapa war leader, sat astride his horse and watched the fighting progress. He was to the east of the rise where most of the remaining soldiers were gathered now. Dead soldiers and horses were scattered all around. There was a thin trail of bodies further to the east, on the other side of the north fork of Medicine Tail Creek. And to his left, on the small rises and in the low gullies toward the river, there were more bodies.

The Hunkpapa warrior guessed that this column of soldiers was larger than the one which had attacked the south end of the encampment. Neither column had fought very well. The advance of the first column had been stopped easily. Once their mounted charge had been turned aside, the encampment was safe. Or perhaps, Gall wondered, those soldiers had only been a ruse. Perhaps they were to occupy all of the warriors until the other soldier column could charge into the camp. They had paid a high price for their ruse. But these soldiers dying on the hill were paying an even higher price.

The dust clouds began to thin a little. Gunfire from the soldiers' hill was no longer heavy. No longer was there a need for warriors to make daring, reckless charges. The soldiers on the rise were hemmed-in. Their high ground, lying east and west, was being slowly boxed-in from its east end. The end of the soldier lines to the west of the rise was also feeling the press of a hard, deliberate warrior advance.

Warriors moving in from the north side of the soldiers noticed a sudden commotion in the bluecoat ranks. In the midst of sporadic fire, a thin shout floated across the dust and a lone mounted soldier broke from the confusion and noise on the rise. He whipped his horse hard toward the east and managed to pass between some scattered warriors and down into the north fork of the dry Medicine Tail Creek. As the soldier came up out of the cut, several warriors took up the pursuit. The soldier's horse was fast and he leaned low over the animal's neck, making himself a small target. But the pursuit was relentless. Warrior rifles boomed and soon a bullet nicked the galloping horse. As he stumbled, the soldier came up out of the saddle to keep his own balance. A bullet's impact turned him in the saddle before he tumbled forward over the horse's withers. After a short trot, the winded animal stopped and looked back up the slope as the pursuing warriors rode up. The soldier rose to a knee fired wildly, and then was cut down for good.

West beyond the end of the soldier lines, Crazy Horse sensed the fighting was nearly over. On the rise, the beleaguered soldiers were fewer and fewer. Most of their horses were gone, stampeded away by young warriors and a few daring boys. Many, many horses were dead. Some horses had been killed by the soldiers themselves, for barricades to hide behind. The Oglala warrior looked across the slopes and rises, at the power of Sitting Bull's vision. A vision which gave the power of the whirlwind to the hearts of Lakota and Cheyenne warriors.

Since the first attack, sometime after mid-day, Crazy Horse had seen many brave things done. He had seen a young warrior ride into a deadly hail of soldier bullets to rescue a brother-friend, and carry him off to safety across the withers of his mount. He had watched an old warrior calmly nock arrows and send them hissing at the soldier lines, even as bullets tore into the earth around him. And then there was the Hunkpapa warrior, Gall. A warrior who put aside his own grief to fight like a wounded bear, knowing that only a dark, silent lodge awaited his return.

Truly, this victory was meant to be. These soldiers had come here to die. Whatever else might have crossed their life paths before now, they had been meant to come to this high place to die. But Crazy Horse could find no softening in his heart for them. He remembered the Grattan Fight, where a wise old Sicangu had died because of a young soldier leader's impetuous reach for glory. He thought of the Blue Water, where many Sicangu relatives had died. And there was Sand Creek and the Washita River.

These were remembrances which brought tears to the eyes of the strongest Cheyenne warriors. Still, this day was no atonement.

There could be no such thing, ever, for all of the human beings killed by soldier bullets and soldier hatred. But perhaps now the Lakota and Cheyenne could gather their power and drive the whites away. Yes. Other whites must learn of the power of the Lakota. As on this day, these soldiers did. Soldiers who had fallen on the grassy river meadow, in the trees along the river, and on the dusty slopes above the river crossing as they ran in retreat. Soldiers who had fallen on the ridges and slopes above the Greasy Grass. Soldiers who fought in confused little groups, like ducks brought down by the hail. Floundering here and there, as if knowing that the only end to this day for them was death.

Gunfire from the soldier rise was very thin. Only a small knot of them were left now, bunched together in a dark pile, fading in and out of the lines of dust floating across the slopes. War cries split the air and mounted warriors swooped toward the soldiers from all directions. A sudden flood washing over the last remnants of an island. Then it was over. Soldier guns were silent.

A sudden quieting fell upon the gullies and ridges above the Greasy Grass River. Warriors moved about, fighting lust still burning in their eyes, not believing it was over. Not believing the sight of so many soldier bodies. So many. All scattered like leaves before a whirlwind.

A drawing by Chief Red Horse of the battle at the Little Bighorn.
It shows that truly the vision of "Soldiers Falling into Camp"
had become reality.
Courtesy of the Smithsonian Insititution.

Colonel F. W. Benteen, 7th Cavalry, U.S. Army, smoking a pipe.
Courtesy of the Denver Public Library,
photo by D. F. Barry, taken sometime between 1874 & 1898,
Call Number: B-299.

CHAPTER 18

Benteen

A contemptuous anger hardened the ruddy planes of Captain Frederick W. Benteen's face, as he didn't like being played the fool. Down here in the southern reaches of the valley all his three companies had scared up were scatterings of deer, and a few game birds, while out front was a patrol headed by Lieutenant Gibson, presently someplace westerly amongst a brace of rugged hills.

By Benteen's estimate, an opinion shared by the other company commanders, they'd gone around twelve to fifteen miles. Hard to tell, he mused, as some hills were so rugged it had forced them to keep to narrow, torturous ravines. Adding to the difficulty was the rocky ground being hard on the horses, and many had become jaded and fallen behind.

Benteen's grudging anger was still there when he came onto a high ridge and halted his command to make an observation. Through his field glass he took in the southern reaches of the valley. But downstream and northerly his view was obscured by jutting promontories, and he could just see pieces of the river below high bluffs. He turned sullen eyes upon Lieutenant Godfrey.

"That Sioux camp is way to the north. Just like Custer to leave us down here chasing shadows."

"I'd say," ventured Godfrey, "we're wandering among these hills without any possibility of accomplishing anything."

Benteen spoke around his briar pipe, "Gibson should be at the river, maybe heading back. In my judgment our only recourse is to head north and pick up the trail followed by the Regiment."

"There, sir, the patrol …"

Since the patrol was still a couple of miles to the west, Benteen got his column moving. He fished out a wooden match and lit his pipe. Soothing his temper somewhat was the lack of any wind, generally a force to be reckoned with.

A bitter thought: Reno should have commanded, not that vain-glorious Custer. The major would have kept the Regiment together, since even one so arrogantly blind as Custer ought to have realized that they were heading into trouble. Custer's consumed by his political ambitions. For sure the country'll go to hell if he ascends to the White House. He kept the column at a walk upon the arrival of Gibson's patrol.

Gibson, dusty and sweating, reported, "Seen nary a soul, Captain Benteen. Lot of dust further north along the river though."

"Where we should be now."

The horse ridden by Benteen was a fast walker, and on the move now, there were times the column had to trot in order to keep pace. They kept skirting low hills, the troopers eyeing the rounded crests or taking hard looks down draws, but all in vain it seemed. The rising heat was another worry. Some of the men had availed themselves of straw hats sold by the sutler aboard the riverboat *Far West*.

While at the head of the column, his shaggy gray hair damp with sweat, Benteen veered onto the main Indian trail taken by the Regiment.

Now a rider overtook them from the east, Boston Custer, who had a cheerful wave for everyone. "Howdy, Lieutenant Edgerly."

"Boston, going AWOL, I see. How far back is the pack train?"

"About three miles." Then Boston Custer was cantering ahead of the column and away.

With a deliberate aloofness Benteen had kept quiet, as he kept his column moving at a walk. A family gathering of the Custers, he mused bitterly, has no place on a military expedition. Upon coming over a rise, he cast away thoughts of the man he despised, for here there was a spring hole, the source of a small stream of running water. The order went down the line for the troopers to water their horses.

"What do you make of it?"

As he dismounted, Benteen looked back at Lieutenant Godfrey gazing questioningly to the northwest, and Benteen said, "Your ears are better than mine. But I'd say the Regiment is engaged." His eyes contained a noncommittal gleam, as if what was happening over there was no cause for hurry. Someone shouted that the pack train was coming in, and Benteen looked to the east to see the first of the mules heading down a distant slope toward the watery morass.

The rest break, as gauged by Benteen, consumed about a half-hour before he gave the order to mount up, and to his orderly, "Once those mules catch the scent of water I don't want to be within a mile of them."

On the move, and about a mile down the trail, a lot of the men were twisting to look back at several mules that had torn loose from the pack train and were tearing for the spring, strewing supplies out of packs coming loose. Then Benteen's trumpeter called out that a rider was coming in hard from the northwest.

Upon sighting Benteen's column, Sergeant Kanipe slanted more to the south. He drew up his sweating horse and threw

Benteen a quick salute. "I've got verbal orders from Custer that he needs the pack train."

Benteen waved an indifferent arm. "Back at that spring you'll find Captain McDougall and his mules." He stared after the sergeant reining away, and the look Benteen threw Lieutenant Godfrey was that it was none of their affair.

Distantly came Kanipe's jubilant shout, "We've got them now, boys!"

As Lieutenant Godfrey dropped back to hook up with his K troop, Benteen and his adjutant picked up the gait to get a hundred yards out front of the column. As for Godfrey, he was puzzled over Benteen's abject attitude. The presence of the courier meant a fight was eminent or even that Custer had attacked. He heard the rattling of hooves on rocky ground and looked to find it was the captain of D Company easing his horse back into a walk.

Captain Thomas Benton Weir said wonderingly, "We know where the hostiles are. Does Benteen?"

"He seems to be a reluctant soldier."

They were fellow Ohioans of the Custers. Weir was a particular partisan of the Regimental commander from his four years in the 3rd Michigan Cavalry — this unit had mutinied against Custer in 1865 — and Weir had testified for the colonel in the court-martial of 1867.

They were as puzzled by Benteen dragging his heels as were the men they commanded. Couldn't be more than two or three miles away from the Little Big Horn River now. As in a faint overture, there came the distant sound as of someone snapping dry wood — gunfire!

Ahead of them, Captain Benteen, with the thick thatch of gray curls filmed with fine dust, held way out in front of the column. He glanced back to check on the column, honed- in on Weir and Godfrey riding together, and snorted disdainfully. As if divining their thoughts, he mused, got no choice but to hold horses nearing the end of their endurance to a walking gait. He would not ask the captains of D and K Companies their opinions. He knew that whatever they said would be slanted to Custer's way of thinking.

Now he squinted his eyes at another cavalryman whipping his horse down the wide and gutted trail. Benteen, raising a gloved hand to halt the column, heard more clearly the popping of weapons, and the Trumpeter Martin was drawing up his lathered horse. Pain was etched on Martin's swarthy face, and blotches of blood stained his trousers where he'd taken a bullet to the hip. He passed to Benteen the abbreviated note from Cooke as Weir and Godfrey swung in, then to witness Benteen reading what he held out loud:

"Benteen come on Big Village Be quick Bring packs W. W. Cooke — Bring Pacs."

"What is happening?" he asked the trumpeter.

One hand pressed to his hip, the trumpeter spoke in a voice heavy with pain. "The Indians are abandoning their village. There is fighting in the village. I think … I think Colonel Custer has made a charge." Tired, gripped with his own pain, he did not pass on to Benteen the information that Custer had further divided his force, that in fact Trumpeter Martin had seen Reno's three companies making the charge down in the floodplain.

"You're lucky it wasn't you," said Benteen. He passed the note to Weir, then he made out another note which he handed to the trumpeter. "Take this to McDougall."

Captain Benteen keened his ears northwesterly, then realized that the sounds of gunfire were tapering off. But even now he did not solicit any advice from Weir or Godfrey. Can't go back for the packs, as those mules can only be pushed so fast. Would take too long getting my column to Custer. The note from Cooke was passed back, and Benteen thrust it into a blouse pocket, to bring the column into a trot.

A mile down-trail, the sound of firing picked up, a continuous barking of rifles, which caused Benteen to pick up the gait, as urgency tightened his face. Foolhardy for Custer to go against so many, he thought. But, if what the trumpeter said was true, the Sioux had been routed. He drew his revolver, gave the order that brought the men he commanded into a gallop, the expectancy in all of them that the victorious Custer was driving the defeated hostiles their way.

The late Major-General Alfred H. Terry, U.S.A.
Wood engraving, Harper's Weekly, December 27, 1890.
Courtesy of the Denver Public Library,
Call number Z-3574.

White Swan, U.S. Army scout, of the Crow Nation.
He stayed with Reno, despite being severely wounded, and was highly praised
by the white soldiers for his extreme courage and fighting prowess.
Courtesy of the Denver Public Library,
photo by Frank A. Rinehart, 1898,
Call Number: X-31265.

CHAPTER 19

The Besieged: The Terror

The terror of bringing his horse down into the soft quicksand of the river channel and the terrible climb up to the bluffs beyond still gripped Major Marcus A. Reno. The Indians had cut them away from the good crossing just to the north, to force them to break upstream to a narrow ford saddled with high river banks taller than a man on horseback.

Whipping his horse around on the prow of the bluff, Reno could still see more of his troopers attempting to escape the trap set by the Sioux. They were strung out in the river, with some still coming out of the brush, firing back at muzzle flashes as mounted Sioux warriors poured down the river from the north. Some troopers, hit by arrow or bullet, tumbled out of their saddles. Blood stained the churning river waters. Dust and smoke seemed to blot out most of what Reno was viewing. Up to him came the agonized screams of cavalrymen beset upon by the Indian horde. And the realization rose in Reno that he'd left behind his dead and wounded.

The major had lost his straw hat to reveal the bandanna

wrapped around his forehead to hold back the sweat, though he seemed unaware of this, and tears were filming his eyes.

He began shouting orders to men scrambling up to safety around him, incoherently, a man gripped with his own shortcomings and personal hell.

Drumming at Reno over the harsh cacophony of battle was the sickening realization that Custer had not supported his attack.

"Where is he, dammit Where is the Regiment?"

Just down-slope Lieutenant Varnum was shouting at the men pouring over the steep edge, "Don't run, men! We've got to go back down there to get our killed and wounded." He ignored a bullet wasping by his face as they swarmed past him, most of them afoot and bewildered and scared.

It came to Reno now that if they were to have any chance at all he needed a defensive position. Dust covered his beard crusted with sweat. He was breathing shallowly, blinking away the tears over the loss of his adjutant, Hodgson, and the loss so many others. His searching eyes picked out a knob on the bluff topped by a shallow depression.

"Doc ... Porter," he shouted, "over there, take your wounded over to that knob! And you others, put your horses there too! Captain!

Captain Myles Moylan detached himself from a small body of soldiers spread-eagled along the edge of the bluff overlooking the river below, to have Reno place him in charge of the wounded. "Moylan, there'll be a lot more. Shouldn't have happened ..."

As more soldiers swarmed onto the top of the bluff, Reno began deploying them in defensive positions, and they began digging with the few utensils they carried, knives and tin cups, at the hard gravelly earth.

He swung around, yelling as he headed toward a torn banner just placed on the knob by Doctor Porter, "Moylan, send someone to find the pack train!"

A trooper screamed, clutched at his back, fell to kick spasmodically, and even as the trooper lay dying the officers and men and Reno realized they were being fired on from the east.

"That ridge yonder, some five-hundred yards away!"

Now gunfire not only came from that ridge but from the north and northwest, with Major Reno acutely aware that they were being encircled. The thought of what would happen then made him break over to his horse tethered with others in a circle around the field hospital. He found his canteen, let the whiskey gorge into his mouth, the biting sting of it warm to his belly.

Reno was appalled at what had happened, in this his baptism of fire against the Indians. Even back in the Rosebud these uncertainties had gripped him. Now, to be Custer's scapegoat, to be the only one attacking a far superior force. He shuddered inwardly. There came images of what had happened to the Arikara, Bloody Knife. He took another desperate drink, as he took notice of more soldiers trickling onto the bluff. Around him the battle went on, guns hammering to answer guns, muffled screams of men being hit, slugs slamming into horses, and always this damnable heat boiling out of a clear sky.

He looked around for his bugler as he corked his canteen. He saw instead some errant bullets scouring into the dusty ground. Then he saw a soldier, one of the new recruits, staggering blindly into the perimeter. Could be no more than seventeen, with half his scalp torn away to hang over his forehead. And Reno yelled, "Get that man over to the field hospital!" He turned to find Lieutenant Wallace of G Company coming in at a crouch.

"We're running out of ammunition."

Reno took this in, realizing that instead of calming him down, the whiskey had only fanned the flames of his uncertainties. He snapped, "Each man had a hundred rounds?"

"And, sir, we need to re-deploy some of the men."

"I'm commanding here," he shot back. He looked around

again. His adjutant, dead, and where were DeRudio and some of the more experienced officers? Over the yammering of rifles he heard a cheer going up, men rising to point southerly at cavalrymen coming in at a gallop. Adding to Reno's confusion were shouts that it was Custer's Regiment coming to their rescue, and then Reno broke toward his horse, having recognized one of them from far out as being Captain Benteen. With the column coming in from the south some of the sniping fire from the east cut away. Major Marcus Reno whipped his tired horse to intercept Benteen. There was fury in Reno's eyes now at what he felt was their commander's failure to support them.

"Where's Custer?"

Reno exploded: "I don't know! I lost a lot of men down there!"

"Here's a message I received from Cooke, to bring the packs." It was here that Benteen realized that Major Reno was having a bad time with this, and Benteen led his column into the defensive perimeter. There'd been the faint smell of whiskey, and as they were friends, he let this slip away.

Another worry was that from the higher bluffs to the southeast he had taken in what he estimated to be about a thousand Sioux warriors milling about on the floodplain west of the river, and some of Reno's command still struggling up out of that deathtrap. He knew it wouldn't be too much longer before those same Indians would be swarming up here, and he began issuing orders despite Reno's close presence.

"Godfrey, dismount your troop and form them in a skirmish line on the bluffs toward the river."

"How far back is the pack train?"

"It was close behind us, Marcus."

Reno waved Lieutenant Hare over and said, "Get mounted and try to hurry up and reach the pack train."

"Yessir, but my horse just won't cut it."

"Take mine, Lieutenant," said Godfrey as he held out the reins.

Swinging into the saddle, Hare called back, "We had a big fight in the bottoms and got whipped." Then he was out of the perimeter and spurring southerly.

Benteen, his teeth clamped around his briar pipe, shook his head at what he saw on the ridge. In strong but quiet words he suggested to Reno what should be done immediately.

"My men are fresh. I'll put more along the bluff below your position." At a crouch Benteen, and Reno and other officers, went that way, to plan as they gazed into the floodplain.

Further westward and obscured by huge clouds of dust stirred the huge pony herd of the Sioux. Closer one could see the entanglement of brush and trees along the Little Big Horn snaking toward the encampment. Another danger, Benteen realized, was the brambled brush choking the draws edging up the bluffs, and sagebrush standing about as tall as a man; from this shelter had come the Sioux who'd scaled the heights and who were dropping arrows among the horses and wounded without having to expose themselves.

"Look at them, hundreds of them!" exclaimed Benteen.

"All itching to lift our scalps," added Reno.

"But where in blue blazes is Custer?"

Some of the answer came when they began to realize that the force of the Sioux attack was wheeling away, the Sioux bringing their war horses northward through the encampment and close to the bends of the river. This followed a sudden burst of gunfire from someplace to the north. They took in the mounted Indians surging in force across the river at about where Medicine Tail Coulee curled down to it, hundreds of warriors, the faint ki-yipping as they rode striking back at Benteen, Reno, the other officers.

"Jesus Christ, Wallace, hear that — and that ?"

"Custer is giving it to them hot," opined Lieutenant Wallace.

There issued a general discussion over what was happening, some of them agreeing that the command ought to do something or Custer would be after Reno with a sharp stick. Reno cut this short by saying, "We'll not move until the packs are up."

Lieutenant Weir, a fellow Ohioan of Custer's, knew the time to move out was now. There was this dread in him that all was not going well with the Regiment. He watched Reno walk away. Reno got up a detail of about a dozen troopers and Doc Porter, with Reno announcing that they were going down to try to recover the body of Lieutenant Hodgson. Weir, frustrated and a bit angry, fell into step with Captain Benteen.

"Can't Reno grasp the situation?"

"Just as much to blame," said Benteen. He lay there, firing at distant targets of opportunity, hearing to his dismay the sounds of battle drifting down from the north, punching looks back across the perimeter.

When Reno and the others appeared, Weir crouched up to head that way.

Major Reno, as he dismissed the troopers, said to Doc Porter, "All I could recover were Hodgson's class ring and this gold bar pin. Fred, it never should have happened . . ."

Benteen, having come over, said contemptuously, "Glory is everything to that damned Custer. So, Marcus, don't blame yourself for what happened."

"Major," Weir said sharply, "I want to take my company and make a reconnaissance downstream."

"Permission denied!"

"This, sir, borders on cowardice."

"I command here!" screamed Reno through widening eyes. He pointed an accusing finger at Weir. "You'll take orders like everyone else, or ..."

"Now," Weir went on recklessly, "is not the time for indecision. Which, Reno, seems to be your strong suit. Whether the pair of you like it or not I'm heading my company downstream."

"Do that and I'll see you're court-martialed!"

Weir swung back, said calmly, "Gentlemen, the honor of the Regiment is at stake. They are badly outnumbered … badly in need of our support …" He left behind a sorrowing shake of his head as he spun around to dogtrot at a crouch back to his company, a bullet nipping at his dusty boot. "Lo'tenant, I'll take my orderly and head for that high bluff directly to the north." Now Weir swung toward the picket line followed by his orderly.

This meant to Lieutenant Edgerly that D Company had been ordered to move into the fray involving the Regiment, and quickly he shouted his troopers off the line and toward their saddled horses. As the company in a column of twos headed after Weir, back of them the lead elements of the pack train appeared.

"Awful quiet to the north," Weir remarked to his orderly as they brought their horses onto an elevation. Westerly and below lay the Sioux encampment, much larger than Weir had anticipated. Some of the dust coming from the floodplain had settled to reveal more of the horse herd.

His orderly exclaimed, "Lordy, there must be at least thirty-thousand horses!"

"At least that," added Weir, but his greater concern was for the deepening silence to the north. North where the air seemed full of dust and smoke rising like scattering clouds.

They could pick out small knots of horsemen; no question but they were Indians. Faintly, they heard the sounds of a few rifles crackling.

"What do you make of it?"

The orderly made no reply as he pointed out that the company was coming in some distance below them, and Weir merely nodded, for he was just beginning to grasp the gravity of their situation. A painful thought: Could the Regiment have been defeated?

"Sir, they've spotted us!"

Swiveling his eyes to the north, Weir took in several Indians pointing in his direction, at first a small wave of warriors spurring their horses into motion, and then seemingly out of nowhere a vast horde of mounted Sioux appeared, thousands Weir estimated quickly in the fear of the moment surging up as of a river overflowing its banks. It was only now the realization sank in that something terrible had happened to the Regiment. Together with the orderly he reined down the slope, shouting to his company, "I believe something has happened to Custer! Now they're headed our way! Too many for us, thousands! We're heading back!"

* * * * * * * *

Once again Captain Frederick W. Benteen had usurped the battalion commander's authority by giving the order to move out. This was shortly after the arrival of the pack train, and perhaps fifteen minutes after the departure the Weir's D troop.

But even in this need for haste, Major Reno wasn't ready when Benteen brought his three companies in the wake of the trail taken by Weir. When Reno finally moved out, the pack train and some of the wounded remained behind, and Reno's concern now was for the troopers forced to go on foot. He was just becoming aware of the deep silence coming not only from the floodplain but also from the north. As advised by Benteen, he had sent Lieutenant Hare after D troop, with Hare to report back immediately with an assessment of the situation.

While under Benteen's steadying influence, some of Marcus Reno's self-assurance was coming back. But this in no way allayed his anger at Custer's betrayal.

About a mile out and about that distance ahead of Reno's command, Captain Benteen remarked that he couldn't see any presence of Weir's D troop, either on the bluff or the rolling flats below, and Benteen said to his adjutant, "Could mean Weir has hooked up with the Regiment."

"Seems we've beaten them, sir."

"To the glory of Custer," he said scornfully, and adding in a dry undertone, "but somehow I expect the worst."

Barely had he spoken than a fresh volley of rifle-fire came from the hidden ridges to the north. Uncertain of what was occurring, Benteen held his column to a dogtrot. Now he was approaching the bluff recently vacated by Weir and his orderly, and it was now that D troop came spilling over a rise in some semblance of march as they galloped their tired mounts. With them was Lieutenant Hare, yelling something, and with excitement shining in his eyes.

"… All of them … thousands … heading this way…!"

Immediately Benteen gave the command to wheel about, with the captain galloping his horse toward Reno's command. Within moments he was there, to draw up by Reno, and together with Reno, and with everyone else in the column, their eyes slid in horrified fascination to what was coming at them from the north.

Reno found his voice. "They'll overrun us unless … unless we find a defensive position. Custer … the others?"

"Not even Custer could stand against that," Benteen lashed out. "Bugler, sound retreat! Back … back to where we left the pack train!"

It was an orderly retreat, some of the companies hanging back to return fire of the Sioux. There was no time to think of what had happened to the Regiment. Except and even through his fear of what was happening came the dark thoughts of Reno: Custer must have headed up north to find Gibbon, Terry.

Then, for everyone, there were only thoughts of survival as the retreating cavalrymen began pouring into the perimeter.

Battlefield, east side of Reno hill, 1886.
Reenactment of Battle at Little Bighorn, taken during Tenth Anniversary
and Reunion on June 25, 1886.
A large group of soldiers and Native-Americans, some on horseback and others
standing in distant center background. Note the actual battlefield debris
of horse bones still visible ten years after the original event.
Courtesy of the Denver Public Library,
photograph taken by D. F. Barry,
Call Number: B-808.

CHAPTER 20

Soldiers on the Hill

People in the camps felt the battle come to an end. Then the victory cries floated down the slopes and across the river. Some gunfire, too. Shots coming here and there in a scattered pattern. Victory shots. And from warriors moving quickly among the soldiers, shooting into bodies with captured revolvers. Word once again spread like a wildfire through the camps. The soldiers had been defeated, driven away.

People moved toward the river crossings to join the warriors on the slopes. Some rode. Most walked or ran. Many were anxious to make sure that their men were safe and unharmed. Others, knowing that there would be dead and wounded warriors, rode or led horses dragging empty travois. A few warriors were just now galloping in from the south. They had been helping to contain the soldiers who had retreated across the river to the bluffs, after that attack had failed.

Everyone knew, or sensed, that the Lakota and Cheyenne warriors had gained a quick victory. The fighting across the river

189

with the second column of soldiers had not lasted long. Not long at all. But as people reached the now quieter battlefield, most were stunned into silence. No soldiers had been left alive. They lay scattered, like dead leaves caught in a wind and then dropped. And in hearts filled with the flush of victory, there was no pity for such an enemy. Even those caught in the most pitiful or laughable poses of death evoked only burning stares of contempt. Contempt for the killers of women and children.

A cry erupted from near the rise where the last of the soldiers had died. It started a commotion. Warriors ran up, weapons ready. But there was no danger. Two Cheyenne women had recognized one of the dead soldiers as others were stripping the body. Creeping Panther, the Arikara called him. To the Lakota he was Long Hair. Long Hair! Ah, yes! He who had led his soldiers in a dawn attack on a sleeping Cheyenne village on the Washita River. A peaceful encampment, flying the bluecoat nation's flag to show that their hearts were not for war.

Over a hundred Cheyenne, mostly women and children, had died that morning. Those who survived had been taken captive. The Washita River was a bitter memory for the Cheyenne. Now, the white man who had led the soldiers there was lying dead on a ridge above the Greasy Grass. Dead, because he tried to attack another encampment. Dead, because Cheyenne and Lakota warriors were much harder to kill than women and children. Cheyenne victory cries pierced the hot summer sky. The Washita had been avenged. Those who had died there could not be brought back. But he who had killed them could no longer recount his deed. This day and this victory would be one long remembered.

A Lakota warrior pushed through the crowd of joyous Cheyenne. The news had aroused his curiosity. If Long Hair had been killed here, then perhaps another soldier leader with the same white name was here, too. Rain In The Face looked carefully at each dead soldier on the rise. And his curiosity was soon laid to rest. Not far from the body of Long Hair was one he recognized. Even in death, this soldier could not hide. This was the soldier leader who had bound Rain In The Face in chains and had taken him to the place called Fort Abraham Lincoln.

There, because of lies about the Hunkpapa warrior killing two white men, he had been imprisoned. But it was not that which drove the warrior to seek revenge. It was the beating. The soldier leader had beaten him as others held his arms. Now that soldier lay dead at his feet. Rain In The Face's only regret was that he had not killed this bluecoat. The warrior drew his knife and slashed open the man's belly. Intestines rolled out. "Now," Rain In The Face said, "You can carry your bowels in your hands as you wander through the next life!" he spat at the dead face and turned away, disdaining the scalp. He would not stain his hands with the blood of such an unworthy enemy.

When the one known as Long Hair had been recognized, the women reached for their skinning knives. These soldiers, these killers of women and children had much to answer for. They would answer for it in the next life. Upper arms were slashed to the bone. Dead fingers were cut off. And some private parts, too. Even Long Hair did not escape this insult. Cheyenne women opened his ears with their bone awls. On the other side, he would forever hear the screams of women and children.

The sun was still high and it beamed hot. By now hundreds of people wandered the battlefield. Dead soldiers were stripped of their clothing, and dead horses were unsaddled. The hot afternoon air was quick to darken the blood of the dead.

Women and children probed the draws and rises, looking for dead and wounded warriors. They found more wounded than dead. All were loaded onto pony drags and taken back to camps.

Gall and Crazy Horse sent several scouts to the north, east, and west to see if other soldier columns might be approaching, and also to look for any soldiers who might have escaped through the dust. After a time, even as the sun sought the western horizon, only the dead soldiers and horses were on the rises and gullies above the river. With the victors back in their camps, the place above the river was only a field of death. Silence lay like a heavy burial robe, with only the occasional screech of the buzzard to split the stillness. And those followers of death were not long in coming to fulfill their purpose. To cleanse the land. They rode in on the same hot breezes which had carried to them the scent of death. On dark, outspread wings they slid to the dust. They shuffled among the bodies, their dark, hunched shapes a contrast to the still, pale forms laying open to the merciless sun and the slash of talon and beak.

A long, hard ride from the stillness near Medicine Tail Creek, and on the same side of the river, warriors crouched under shrubs and in the sparse shade of shallow, narrow ravines. They were hiding more from the sun than from the soldiers barricaded on the flat beyond the bluff's rim.

In spite of their costly retreat through the trees, across the river, and up the face of the bluffs, many soldiers from the first attack managed to reach the safety of the bluffs. There they were joined by another column riding in hard from the south.

The soldiers formed an attack toward warriors moving up the bluffs, but it was only a feint to cover some bluecoat stragglers still scrambling up the face of the bluff. Once all the soldiers were on the rim, some of the warriors pursuing the retreat moved up the slopes and hid themselves.

After a long lull, soldiers in large and small groups started back down the slopes. Some carried canteens and some hurried toward the bodies of fallen bluecoats.

Two warriors knelt against the bank of a narrow gully, peering between the stalks of dead sage. Soldiers were moving south of their position toward the water. One of the warriors, a Miniconju with a good repeating rifle, brought down a soldier. The others scattered and dashed for the river, some of them dropping behind the river's edge, though it was only as high as to a man's ankle. They hurriedly filled the canteens even as bullets kicked up around them. Lakota gunfire grew heavier and forced the soldiers away from the water, and up the slope to better cover. Along the way, some were hit. Some of the canteens were shot away as well, water spilling as the soldiers ran.

A line of soldiers fired from the bluffs, though it was plain that they couldn't see the warrior positions. Bullets hit closer to the running soldiers than to the warriors. The firing from the edge of the bluffs came faster as more soldiers joined in the fight. It was enough to help those scrambling up the steep sides to reach the rim. After that, the firing slowed and then stopped altogether.

Messengers had come from the camps, carrying word to the warriors engaging the bluff soldiers. The attack on the north end of the camp had been turned aside. All of the soldiers in that large column had been killed. Those bluecoats on the bluff must be kept from moving closer to the encampment, the messengers said.

All of the soldiers in one column killed! That was news to quicken the heart. It must have been a good, hot fight, more than one warrior said. And some expressed disappointment at not being part of it. But there was much yet to do here. A new column had joined those who had retreated up the bluff. There were still soldiers to worry about. And there was no way to know how many soldiers were beyond the bluffs now. For a time, they should be watched closely, someone decided. Perhaps a small group of warriors could sneak in close.

"Hau!" a young warrior said, eyes flashing. "I will go!"

Several others joined in quickly. It was decided. The new scouts would sneak in as close to the soldiers as they could. "We will signal if the soldiers try to break away or move toward the encampment," one of the scouts said. "A fire-arrow down toward the river. Those of you waiting below should keep a sharp lookout, too. These soldiers on the hill could be strong enough to move on the camps. Watch for the signal!"

Now, several pairs of warriors were scattered about. Some had moved over the edge of the bluff. Others were just below it. All well hidden, covered with dust or cut shrubs. The sun long stayed high, this summer day. But if it was difficult for the scouts, it was even more so for the soldiers in the open with no shade.

Soon, the telltale noises of large numbers of mounted horsemen moving together was plainly heard. And they were moving north, along the ridges above the river. Two warriors slid back down the steep slope into a deep sheltering gully, and quickly prepared a fire-arrow. Sent by a strong, sinew-backed bow, it flew very high into the air. It carried far, nearly halfway to the river, and it trailed smoke as it hissed earthward. One of the warriors hiding in the draws at the river bottom jumped from his shelter and sprinted along the water's edge. He shouted a message to some who were hiding in the trees.

"Soldiers!" Moving north along the ridge!"

Word was relayed quickly. Mounted warriors moving along the river, and some who were resting their horses in the willows were quick to spot the soldier column along the ridge. They responded, immediately.

At least two or three hundred rode to cut off the bluecoats, moving so rapidly that they nearly caught the soldiers separated in two thin columns. The column furthest to the north was slow to turn. Some of the lead warriors fired, even though they were at the edge of their weapons' accurate range. But at least one soldier fell wounded, and was left behind as the rest galloped back to the barricades on the flat beyond the bluffs. The hard-charging warriors closed the gap and poured heavy fire into the end of the departing column.

When the soldiers reached the bluffs and returned some organized firing, the warriors slowed their charge and turned. They moved out along the washes and rises all around the soldier position on the bluff top. Their movement was slow and deliberate, sizing up the soldiers even as they moved themselves into a long, long half-circle, north and east around the bluecoats. Finally, the Lakota and Cheyenne had the soldier hill completely surrounded. More and more warriors arrived from the camps. But many were still in the camps, staying behind just in case more soldiers arrived from some unexpected direction. Still, it was plain that most of the able warriors were on the hot dusty hills around the soldiers. Some of them were preparing for their third battle since the sun was halfway in the sky. A lifetime ago, it seemed.

Crazy Horse, on yet another fresh horse, watched the soldiers in the distance. Like ants. Black specks inside the dust raised by their horses. The Oglala looked along the wide curving line of warriors. He was glad to see so many. Perhaps as many as had ridden against Three Stars on the Rosebud. He knew that those who met and turned away the first attack on this day were not nearly half as many. That was also true of the second attack. But now they were gathered in stronger numbers, though there were many wounded and some in the camps standing guard. And it was time to finish this thing, especially since there were enough warriors to do it.

Warriors began to creep toward the soldier barricades, crouching low and using gopher holes and clumps of grass for cover. The soldiers opened fire, hot and heavy. Warriors responded, volley for volley, shot for shot. Some crawled very close before firing. A few of them went too close and were quickly driven back. Here and there, a warrior paid dearly for his daring. Many warriors crept to within bow range and lifted arrows in a high, lazy arc to drop them in among the horses and soldiers behind a low rise or a thick clump of soapweed. Older warriors with guns took up positions like the bowmen, squeezing off a shot each time a soldier head was visible.

Some groups of soldiers took up positions away from the barricades, but were quick to fall back as mounted warriors rode at them. With each charge the warriors swung in closer and closer to the soldiers, riding low over their horses' withers. Some riding to the offside of the horse, holding on with only a heel and a loose neck rope, and firing from beneath the neck of the galloping animal. Though some horses were hit, the rider often escaped unhurt. After a few such daring charges, the soldiers stayed behind their cover, unwilling to face mounted warriors in the open.

Time wore on and the fighting settled into a bitter, shot for shot struggle. But the soldiers were well entrenched and their supply of bullets was clearly greater. For every shot from a hidden sniper, the bluecoats returned several. And though the soldiers could not be dislodged from their sheltering barricade, the Lakota and Cheyenne had accomplished their purpose once again.

The encampment was safe. As the sun dipped toward the west and the shadows grew longer, word reached Crazy Horse, Gall, and the other war leaders gathered on a rise far to the north of the soldiers. Warriors were using up their bullets. The message brought a quick response. It was time to return to the encampment. Only a small force would be left to guard the soldiers. But nearly every warrior knew that the soldiers had lost their spirit for fighting. If they did anything during the night, it would be to escape. Even that would not be easy, because of their wounded.

Messengers were sent among the warriors. Soon after, the firing began to thin until at last an uneasy silence fell. The Lakota and Cheyenne withdrew more cautiously than they had advanced. No one wanted to be hurt or die because of a small carelessness, especially after having lived through day. Besides, there would be another day. Time enough to finish these soldiers. It would be good for the bluecoats to spend their last night of life thinking about the power of the Lakota. Night guards were chosen and signals agreed upon, just in case the soldiers did try something. Then the warriors rode away, without so much as a single parting shot from the soldiers.

The mood in the great encampment was one of a sense of

strength. Yet there was a somberness, also. Though the attacking soldiers had been beaten back, there was the reality of their attacks. They had been brave enough, or foolish enough, to attack a large and powerful gathering. Of the two, foolishness was a greater worry. One who was brave was also, for the most part wise. One who was foolish could not be counted on to think wisely. And of all the ways in which the white man thought and acted, it was foolishness which guided him most often. That was the worry. There were many, many whites. They could afford to lose many soldiers to foolishness. As they had today. But there were only a few people of the Earth. Only a few true human beings. And they needed to be wise, as well as brave.

The dark western horizon slowly covered the face of the sun like an old woman slowly covering her head with the mourning robe. After the warriors returned from the last fight on the bluffs, a few of them celebrated. But a quietness lay over the camp circles. The soldiers had come in strength, perhaps foolishly thinking that victory was the reward of bluster and noise. Perhaps thinking that all Lakota and Cheyenne camps could be defeated as easily as on the Washita and the Little Powder.

They could not know that the Lakota and Cheyenne warriors were assured of victory long before this day's fights. Sitting Bull's great vision, given in return for his sacrifice of flesh and pain, had strengthened the hearts of the warriors. But the victory they gained this day did not come without cost. Many warriors had been hurt in the battles. Some had died. Though the number of warrior dead were far, far fewer than the soldiers killed, to each grieving family the loss was the heaviest of burdens. Even now, as the western sky darkened into evening, the mourners prepared their dead for the burial scaffolds. A mother, wife, or a grandmother sought comfort in the knowledge that her warrior had willingly turned his steps onto the path of many, many warriors before him. But it did not ease the pain. Knowing, that for her son, or husband, or grandson, a warrior's death in the defense of his people was the highest of honors, did little to stem the flow of tears. And those who would celebrate did so quietly in deference to those in whose lodges death was a visitor, knowing that the victory truly belonged to those who had given everything for it. Here and there, deep in the shadowy folds of the camps, an honoring song could be heard. And with each, all who could hear it paused to listen. Though they may not have known him for whom it was sung. It was enough that he had died for the people.

At a brush shelter near the river, east of the Sicangu camp, a young man sat back and stared at the small fire he had started. Behind him, to the west, between the tall lodge poles and the spreading arms of the tall cottonwoods, the sun sent its last red arrows of light from behind the dark rim of the Earth. Night had come. Hunger bothered his belly but he made no move to satisfy it. There was a greater concern. The sun had still been high when last he saw his cousin. A mourner's long, keening wail from somewhere close by only deepened his worry. After he had found help to bring the two wounded warriors back into the encampment, White Tail Feather had returned to the timber to search for his cousin. He found other wounded warriors and helped to take them to the camps. But Bear was nowhere to be seen.

Night settled in and there was much activity in the camps. The fighting blood, worked to a fever pitch, took long to cool. Warriors moved about, leading to fresh mounts to picket outside the lodge while others took up guard positions at the edge of the camps. Some carried new soldier rifles. Small groups bunched here and there as individuals talked in subdued excitement about their part in the fighting. Those with families stayed close to their lodges, relieved that their woman and children were safe. Still others wanted the quiet security of home and family, to help sort out all that had happened this day.

A quick, sharp rustling through the grass turned White

Feather Tail's head. Bear, tall, slender, and covered with dust, moved into the soft firelight. "I am glad to see you, cousin," he said, fatigue in his voice.

White Feather Tail gazed long at his cousin, even as the other sat down close to the fire. Fatigue covered his face with dark hues. An elbow was skinned. Leggings were torn and he wore only one moccasin. But it was the distant emptiness in his cousin's eyes which caught and held White Feather Tail's attention. More than the new soldier rifle.

"It is good to see you," he replied.

Bear lifted his tired eyes to his cousin's face, and gestured toward the darkness. "The soldiers seem to be digging in. It is hard to see what they are doing now. But we could hear them. Their injured ones cry out now and then. And some of their friends keep trying to reach the water in the darkness, to take some back to the bluff. I think the soldiers are in a bad way. I think … I think they are sorry they came here today." He looked off into the darkness as his last words faded a little.

White Feather Tail cleared his throat. There would be time, he hoped, for each of them to talk of what they had seen today. And what it made them feel. He knew that his cousin must have been up very close to the soldiers now on the hill, close enough to hear what they were doing. That was a very strong and brave thing for them to do. He wanted to hear more about it, even if it made him feel small. All he had done was haul injured men back to the camps. In the coming days, there would be time for talking. Now, he was hungry. "I can find some food, if you are hungry," he offered.

Bear looked up and nodded. "That would be good. And I think we should find some food and take it up to the men watching the soldiers. Water, too. Some of them have not had water since the soldiers first came."

Two women approached in the firelight, in time to hear the

young warriors' words. "We have food," one of them said. "Some of the families back in the camps prepared the food, for the warriors. Please come, and eat. We have more than enough in our lodge. And we can put some together for you to take up to the hills."

Bear and White Feather Tail came to their feet. One of the women had her hair cut short. And there were gashes on her forearms. The other had daubed her face with wet ashes. All of these things were signs of mourning. In a soft reply to the questioning glances of the two of the two young warriors, one of them said, "It was my brother." The one who spoke was the one who had gashed her arms and cut her hair.

"And he was my cousin," said the other.

"Thank you, for the offer," White Feather Tail finally said. He knew well that those in mourning must be careful of their thoughts and behavior for four days. Because, as everyone knew, it would be how they would think and act for the rest of their lives. Now, these women were doing a very strong thing. They were helping others, because they were in mourning.

The cousins followed the two women to a lodge in the east edge of the Oglala camp. They were fed, and the women of the lodge prepared packs of food to be taken up to the warriors keeping watch over the soldiers. Skins of water were also provided. Someone quietly handed Bear a pair of moccasins. Though death had come to this lodge, the family did not withdraw from relatives and friends in its grief. Instead, they prepared food and invited warriors to eat. Those things were not charity, however. They were done to honor their memories of one who would never sit in the lodge again, and to allow others to share their loss.

Back at their own camp, Bear helped White Feather Tail tie the food packs and water skins over the withers of their only horse. White Feather Tail had not been able to find his mount. As they started for the south end, Bear with his new rifle and White Feather Tail with a fresh supply of arrows, they were glad to see that others were also taking food and water to the warriors on the bluffs. There was little talking as they led the horse through the darkness. Coyotes could be heard all around. Some barked, and some howled mournfully. A fitting end to a day which seemed to last a lifetime.

Photograph of Unknown Remains,
taken at the Little Bighorn Battlefield one year later (1877),
courtesy of the Denver Public Library,
by Herbert A. Coffeen, Publisher, of Sheridan, Wyoming,
Call Number: X-33173.

Battle site at Little Bighorn, Montana, west side of Reno Hill.
In the center, one man holds a horse's reins.
A large group of horseback riders is visible in the distant center.
Courtesy of the Denver Public Library,
photograph taken by D. F. Barry
during the Reunion and 10th Anniversary of Battle (1886),
Call Number: B-541.

CHAPTER 21

The Besieged:
Smoke Rising from the Floodplain

Westerly the darkening sky was a tattered saddle blanket grimed by dust and smoke rising from the floodplain. The thick cloud obscured the setting sun. It seemed brighter to the east to survivors of Custer's 7th Cavalry, exposed as they were on the bluffs above the Little Big Horn. The rattling of gunfire went on and on, but it wasn't so much the return fire from the Sioux but the lack of water which worried Major Marcus Reno.

A tally taken a few minutes ago told of at lest twenty more dead, fifty added to his casualty list. He held down behind a dead horse, alone, as Benteen had gone off to his company. During the dying remnants of the afternoon there'd been a lot of talk between Reno and Benteen over what had happened to Custer's command. Both of them had bitterly denounced their commander.

The perimeter had taken the shape of a horseshoe. Due in to the east were the remnants of three companies, K, D, G, the other companies circling around to guard the bluffs looking down upon the Little Big Horn. Southerly it was Captain Moylan's A troop settled in behind pack saddle breastworks and dead horses and mules, the wounded lying in the only depression on the bluff. For the most part the men were simply stretched out on bare ground and hoping for the best. Those horses and mules still alive were secured in a tight circle, their reins anchored to the legs of dead horses.

Reno looked back of him at the edge of the bluff where his defense was thinnest, the heavier concentration of troopers holding to the north. Then out to the surrounding terrain consisting of a series of small hills and ridges falling away gradually to a ravine. Out of here came a harassing fire from the Sioux. Of more concern to everyone in the perimeter were the higher ridges off to the left; it was from here the heavier fire came. Gazing skyward, Marcus Reno could still make out high-soaring turkey vultures, and he cursed, "Damn, come here to pick the bones of our men." His face wore an anguished scowl, and he would have gone in search of Benteen, but fear of being hit as it dusked held the man commanding the besieged and kept him hunkered low.

* * * * * * * *

The commander of M troop, Captain Thomas French, yelled to one of his troopers, "Private, keep down!"

A warning that came too late as Private Henry Voight felt the impact of a rifle bullet. French was sharing the fears of the men in K company in that a sharpshooter had zeroed-in on them from a high ridge someplace to the north.

From the yells over there French knew the Sioux marksman had killed several troopers. Now his M troop was being worked over.

Twisting onto his side, French warned again, "Keep low or any of us'll be next. Sergeant Ryan, pass the word."

Captain French and his men flattened in more, scanning the distant ridge through the last light of day, French more concerned for his men than himself. Forgotten was this awful thirst or any thoughts of Custer's whereabouts, the chief topic of concern up until now. He snaked a look over his saddle wedged over some empty ammunition boxes, as he reached over cautiously to nudge Sergeant Ryan.

"Think that Sioux has a scope?"

"That … or about the best rifleman I've ever seen."

There came from his troopers the recoil of a few rifles to have slugs plow harmlessly into the distant ridge. Or had they taken out the sharpshooter? There was an immediate response when the fourth man from Sergeant Ryan grunted in pain, and died. Now the third man away from Ryan received a hit, then the second. French yelled, "Ready to lift and fire at that ridge! Now!"

Captain French, the sergeant, and several others rose to put a deadly volley into the height, and dropped down again to embrace the hard earth. Though firing came from other points, the raking fire from the sharpshooter never came again. And as night embraced the bluff, the fear in a lot of them was to expect an attack, but night also exposed the exact point of discharge of Sioux rifles, the troopers honing-in on these red spurts of light. But the darkness aided the Sioux more than the troopers on the bluff, as now small groups of Indians were able to slink in through shadowed low places to within spear or arrow reach … weapons that created no betraying fire.

Captain French, as did other company commanders, sent troopers over to the pack train in search of bullets and something to eat, with others more interested in obtaining water.

"Take over, Ryan," the captain said as he crouched away and went to find Major Reno.

French's search brought him by the knobby depression containing the wounded and to men clustered by the pack train, where he ran into Lieutenant Godfrey, to have Godfrey respond with, "I'm looking for the major too. We need water, bad. It'll mean getting up a detail."

"Reno, he must be aware of this. But where is he?"

There was some more small talk, questions about Custer's whereabouts, then both officers headed out to search the perimeter.

Overhearing the conversation had been a trooper from C Company there foraging for supplies. Now he looked over as Lieutenant Edgerly eased out of the darkness. "Wasn't that Captain French?"

"Yessir," replied the trooper, "in search of our brave Major Reno. Well, he's yonder cowering in his hole. Seems to me the major wants to pull the hole in after him ... if that were humanly ..."

"That's enough, Private," said Edgerly with a mild rebuke. He moved away from the private ripping open a box of rations, and paused when, lifting from the Sioux encampment spread along the floodplain, came the ominous tom-tomming of drums. A sorrowful thought: they're celebrating their victory over Custer. For what Edgerly did not believe was one of the rumors flying about the perimeter that Custer had headed north to find Gibbon.

Lieutenant Edgerly realized that those beating drums didn't signify the Sioux were planning a night attack. He recalled talking some time ago to a Shoshone down in Wyoming, of the Shoshone averring night dews softened the moccasin sole to rock and thorn, and stretched bowstrings so they refused to send arrows at their enemies. "Tomorrow, let's pray the Montana column arrives ..."

It was his contention the lack of water had brought Captain French in search of Reno. The same errand he'd been sent on by the D troop commander. As he headed away from the packs strewn about in the direction pointed out to him by the trooper, distantly he took in heat lightning lancing earthward to the southwest. Here on the bluff the air was filled with static electricity, and dust, and the cries of the wounded, the erratic sounding of weapons. The clouds above him signified rain. When at last he came upon Major Reno, a few raindrops touched down, making a few blots like a bobcat lightfooting across a clearing.

* * * * * * * *

"Not enough to fill a snuff-box," Major Marcus Reno muttered as he left his place of refuge, to bring Edgerly toward the edge of the bluff. "All the water we need is down there."

They stared at the dull glinting river ox-bowing toward the Sioux encampment ablaze with campfires. "Edgerly, I ordered a detail to be formed. Even so, look down there. But those hostiles have piled up dry grass just in case we try for the river, so they spot anyone going down. You, see, Edgerly, I am concerned about my men ... I ..."

Lieutenant Edgerly could smell the whiskey, see the worry in the major's eyes, and he knew that Marcus Reno had some concern for the men he commanded. But he also knew, as did the other officers, that the inadequacies of the battalion commander outweighed everything else. Out of the darkness and to them came Captain Benteen puffing unconcernedly on his briar pipe. There was a civil nod for Edgerly.

"You ever see such a sight before," he said angrily.

Underneath a thin layer of clouds that had slipped in within the half-hour they gazed into the floodplain at the huge campfires made by the Sioux. Warriors were dancing around many of them, their shadows gigantic and leaping away in light flaring up to etch the shadows against the bluffs and ridges. Others on the bluff were taking in the victory dances, the recruits sure that this signified a night attack. The veterans assured them there'd be no attack until morning.

Benteen said, "I've gotten up a water detail. Yes, right about here I'll place four of my best marksmen. Those going for water will sneak down that draw off to our left. Moon's behind those clouds, which should help."

"They're all volunteers?"

"Yes, Marcus," he said around a reassuring smile, "around twenty said they'll give it a go. Several from your company, Edgerly."

At the sound of boots scuffing over the hard ground they turned, and there were four men armed with rifles, and bellying down with empty canteens and camp kettles. Only two wore the broad yellow stripes of a sergeant, as the rest were privates. Edgerly recognized two of them, Goldin and Deitline, then one of the sergeants was bringing his charges southerly off the crown of the bluff to slip into the coulee.

Courage, pondered Edgerly, seemed not to be lacking in these young recruits. He crouched down alongside Reno, with Benteen going down the line where H troop was holding, his words coming clipped clear.

"Concentrate your fire along the far bank if our water detail is spotted. You see a muzzle-flash, keep pouring in shells."

When Benteen came back, he crouched alongside Major Reno, then he brought his pipe down to tap it against a small rock and dislodge the blackened tobacco. Some of the Arikara scouts, those who'd refused to cross the river before, had managed to get through the Sioux lines. After consulting with Reno, Captain Benteen had sent one of them, Forked Horn, and Goose, a wounded Sioux scout, up north in an effort to find Gibbons' column, with Reno refusing Lieutenant Varnum's offer to go along. Even Benteen had accepted the fact something had happened to the Regiment.

At the moment the heat lightning kept revealing the bluffs along the river in a reddish glare, and Benteen pulled out his revolver, knowing it would take something of a miracle for the water detail to have any chance at all.

Edgerly had drawn his revolver, but Reno hadn't, as he said to Benteen, "I'm worried about the pack train."

"Foragers?"

"Those civilians, some of them are nothing but thieves."

He wanted to turn hot on Custer again, but there was Edgerly. So Reno lapsed into silence, mindful of the fact he'd emptied his canteen, and the small keg of whiskey hidden among the supplies.

Fireflies danced in the brush across the river, those dark objects perched amongst the trees, vultures drawn here by this afternoon's battle. Back of the men keeping vigil along the bluff came the sweetish stench caused by blood and the woundings. Dead horses and mules were swelling up, those having been struck by bullets after being killed letting off a sour gaseous smell. Everyone was filmed with dust, aware of the detail trying for the river.

* * * * * * * *

Down in coulee angling toward the Little Big Horn, Sergeant Hutchinson threw up a warning hand when something stirred in the brush across the flowing river. Out of a blacker cloud issued big splattering raindrops, the cloud cutting off the glare of heat lightning. Hutchinson whispered back to the other sergeant with the detail, "Now's the time to hit for the river. But I can't make out what's over there."

"Indians for damned sure," said Sergeant Stanislaus Roy, a kettle in one hand, his service revolver in the other, and as nervous as the privates strung out behind them. His jaw worked over the plug of tobacco tucked in against his cheek, eyes stabbing beyond the river. "Benteen said we'd have covering fire if something happened."

Then he fell silent when both of them discerned the vague form of an Indian holding by a cottonwood, the rain cutting away with a quick finality, as did the Indian, and Hutchinson brought his charges down, down to the lower mouth of the coulee. An arm-signal brought them out onto an exposed section of land running toward the near bank. They spread out and down, dipping kettles and canteens into the life-giving waters. Then again heat lightning cut away the enshrouding darkness, and as it did, rifle-fire and arrows pierced toward them. Return-fire came from up on the bluff, heavier than from the Sioux and Cheyenne.

At the river's edge, a bullet ripped a hole in the canteen held by Private Frank Tolan to tear it out of his hand. But with a calmness born of desperation he managed to fill the camp kettle, as Tolan virtually stared into the muzzle-flashes of rifles seeking to kill him and his companions. Further along a private, Tanner, had just risen up with his camp kettle filled with water, when he took a hit in the stomach and moaned his frightened anguish.

"Back, back!" yelled Sergeant Hutchinson, as he slung an arm around the wounded Tanner, everyone else falling back toward the coulee and firing their revolvers.

Across the river piles of grass sprang into flame to light up the night sky. But fewer and fewer warriors fired at the retreating water detail because of the accuracy of the marksman placed on the bluffs by Captain Benteen.

When at last the water detail came up out of the coulee, the sergeant in charge guided them over to the field hospital.

Shortly thereafter men assigned to get water trickled over from the various companies.

As for Major Marcus Reno, he was profuse in his thanks for Benteen's help. "Fred, you have been a Godsend."

Benteen, with a smile, said, "I could use something stronger than water ..." "Yes, a miracle only one man was wounded."

"It's my recommendation these men get medals," he said, as in step they converged upon the pack train, their presence moving out a couple of civilian drovers, unaware that one of the men standing guard duty there was Private John Burkman, Custer's former orderly.

Burkman stayed in the shadows draping away from stacks of supplies, as once again he took in Major Reno coming back to refill his canteen. "Men are dying of thirst and he's got whiskey," he thought to himself. He hadn't revealed the location of Reno's private whiskey hoard to the other sentries. Unlike certain privileges granted officers, he knew that what Reno was doing violated all the regulations, and it rankled him. Earlier when Reno had showed up he had cursed some drovers away, accusing them of stealing army rations. Easing down on a box of ammunition, John Burkman got a testy look on his face when talk about Custer came to him.

First there was Reno's jeering voice, "I wonder where the Murat of the American army is by this time?"

Benteen joined in Reno's laughter, had some more whiskey from the canteen, and spoke a few disparaging words about the commander of the 7th Cavalry. "Away back in '67, Marcus, was the first time I laid eyes upon Custer. Summoned me to his office, an ordeal. Bragged on and on about his past exploits. But it wasn't until a couple of years later, after the Battle on the Washita. Anyway, you know how I feel ..."

"Come sun-up they'll be hot on us, Fred."

"Hot and trying to finish us as I expect they did that fool Custer." He had a grin. "I'm going to check on my company. Give me about a half-hour, then we'll look in on the other companies." He wanted to tell Reno to lay off the whiskey, but held his peace as he slipped away.

Thoughts of what morning would bring held Major Marcus A. Reno to his seat on a box. He rubbed the nape of his neck, easing some of the pressure he felt, drinking more to chase away the pain and frustrated anger over the death of his adjutant. Ever since sun-up he'd nibbled at the whiskey, but in a way felt immune to it, and a lot of things.

Softer, "Murat of the American army; as damned ambitious, Custer." His words were slurry, and he would have gone on with a rambling tirade against all that had happened had not he become aware of shadowy forms moving in.

He watched, heavy-lidded, as a civilian packer he knew began prying open a box.

Pushing to his feet, Reno started that way, holding onto his canteen and hefting a carbine. He called out drunkenly, "Are the horses tight?"

The packer, a man named Frett, turned to look at the major coming to him, and Frett replied, "Major, I don't understand … just what do you mean?"

Reno barked, "Tight, God damn you, tight!" He struck the packer in the face with the hand holding the canteen, to have whiskey splay over Frett's face and hat. Now Reno brought up the carbine, threatening to do harm to the packer.

It was then that the other packer, Churchill, intervened as he pulled Frett away, blurting out, "Major, all we wanted was some hardtack and saddle blankets. Frett here, someone stole his saddlebags too." He managed to inch the other packer off into the darkness of the perimeter.

Observing this had been Private John Burkman, and wisely he stayed hidden as Major Reno let the rifle clatter onto some boxes, the major refilling his canteen before he wandered off in the direction of the field hospital.

"Knew Reno was a heavy drinker back at the fort," the older Burkman said sorrowfully. "A pity, is all, a damned pity. For the likes of Reno'll be commanding in the morning when the Sioux strike us again. Lord, starting tonight I've turned into a praying man. For Reno, for all of us."

* * * * * * * *

The sustained gunfire that had come from the bluff had penetrated the thorny thickets where four men from Reno's command were holed-up. That afternoon they'd been unable to heed their commander's orders to make for the bluffs after that illadvised charge along the floodplain. The fact they were alive at all was due to the fact that the Sioux had given up beating through the brush along the river for any survivors.

Lieutenant Carlos DeRudio would never forget the sight he'd had out of the brush of Indian women hunting down the

214

wounded troopers, their dying screams as knives and axes cut into their flesh. While around them Sioux warriors had filtered in to send a harassing fire up the bluff. Now in the uncertain and awful darkness of night he said to his companions, "At least they have some water now."

"If only they can hold out until the Montana column gets here," said Private Thomas O'Neil. Hunkered in close to the cavalrymen were two other survivors, the interpreter Girard, and scout Billy Jackson.

Through the brush they could see into the Hunkpapa camp circle, and glimpse some of the celebration that was going on. Down in here they were much closer to Medicine Tail Coulee. They had heard the battle raging this afternoon between Custer's Regiment and the Sioux. When it was over a trumpet had sounded from that general direction, to have their hopes rise. But with the return of the Indians to their encampment and a lot more going in to attack Reno's battalion, they knew the Regiment was no more.

They had discussed breaking across the river, but knew after the water detail had come under attack that Sioux warriors were all around them. All they had were their weapons, their canteens and horses in the hands of the Sioux. A short while before the commotion along the river, Billy Jackson had made it down through weeds to the river to slake his thirst. When things quieted down more, the other would do the same.

DeRudio, from Italy and something of a storyteller, said through his parched throat, "I feel we'll get out of this."

"You mean make a break for the bluffs tonight?"

"Perhaps," he whispered back to Girard. "I figure the hostiles will break away when Gibbon arrives. No sooner than tomorrow though."

Billy Jackson, grandson to Montana's first Indian-trader, Hugh Monroe, and a half-blood Blackfoot, whispered cautiously, "Expect them to attack the battalion at first light. Thought we have no food except for some of these berries, we can get to water. Tonight, I don't think we will make it across the Greasy Grass."

Girard spat out, " Even the Sioux have to sleep."

"Billy's right," said Lieutenant DeRudio. "As the fact is, we're still alive. With what's happened today, sleep's the last thing on the mind of Crazy Horse and his bunch. They have … they have Custer's victory … and come sun-up they'll attack once again." Light from burning piles of grass had penetrated through the mass of thicket, to show the worried look in the Italian's dark brown eyes. He had a square face, a graying mustache, and a goatee. He'd removed his tunic, but still had on the dark blue cap with the crossed sabers just above the black brim.

"If anything," he went on softly, "the army has taught me patience. We are all tired, so for now a little sleep won't hurt. So, my friends, I'll stand the first watch."

Monument to General George Armstrong Custer and his officers,
soldiers and scouts, Battle of Little Bighorn;
monument was completed in 1881; large granite marker in background
with several wooden grave markers and piled stones in foreground.
Photograph by D.F. Barry between 1881 and 1886.
Courtesy of the Denver Public Library,
Call number: B-812

Lieut. J. J. Crittenden, 20th Infantry, Fell Here in Custer Battle, June 25, 1876.
From Photo Taken One Year Later.
Herbert A. Coffeen, Pub., Sheridan, Wyo.

Lieutenant J.J. Crittenden
photograph taken by Herbert A. Coffeen, Publisher, of Sheridan, Wyoming,
one year after the battle (1877),
Courtesy of the Denver Public Library,
Call Number: X-33597.

CHAPTER 22

Toward the Shining Mountains

Dawn lingered in red glows. Then the sun leaped over the horizon, sending a brightness soaring over the hills, gullies, and meadows around the Greasy Grass River. The encampment on the broad valley floor west of the river was already into the rhythms of a new day. Sleepy-eyed boys hurried toward the pony herds, to take their families' horses to water and then to the lodges. Word had been carried through the camp circles before sun-up by strong voiced camp-criers. The people were to move.

Many old men leaders had gathered in the council lodge just after sundown of the day before. They had talked far into the night. They talked about the fighting. About the soldiers dead on the hillsides across the river, and those still alive on the bluffs. Something had to be done about all of them. And anything to be done must be with the safety of the people in mind. Some war leaders came to the council lodge and talked strongly for killing all of the soldiers still on the bluff. Many of the old men leaders didn't agree. One warrior dead was one warrior too many, they said. And the pitiful bunch of bluecoats on the bluff were not together worth an

219

encampment warrior dead or injured. Better to leave them there, the old men said. Those soldiers were harmless now. It was the dead ones on the hills which were more bothersome. And when the sun rose higher and became hotter, they would be even more so. So it would be better to move. The soldiers were not strong enough to follow them. And there were more and more reports of other soldier columns to the north, moving south. Besides, a few of the people had already left the encampment, one old leader pointed out. To move the would be a wise thing. Perhaps toward the Shining Mountains. Summer was still young. With new grass for the horse herds, the people could stay together a little longer. And the hunting in the Shining Mountains was always good.

But though the old men leaders were wise, they could only give advice, could only suggest what the people should do, especially the warriors. Even as they had sat in council, some warriors on the bluffs had briefly opened fire on the soldiers. But they soon broke it off.

And as the camp-criers moved through the circles of lodges, announcing that the people should prepare to move, warriors began to gather and move toward the bluffs. Sharp firing cracked the morning air as some who had been hiding between the river and the bluff top opened fire at the soldiers now being uncovered by the growing light. Soldiers returned the fire, but only now and then. The light showed the warriors, too. And to their own surprise, they could see that many more of them had gathered around the soldiers during the night. Mounted warriors were gathering along the river bottoms close to the camp. They were visible to the warriors below the bluff.

Somewhere on the ridge, south of the soldier barricade, someone opened fire. It quickly turned into many gunshots, like a long, long rapid drumbeat. A new day, a new battle.

Warriors already up the ridges moved to high points, some sniping long-range while others repeated the tactics of the previous afternoon. Moving in close, keeping to the gullies and hiding behind knolls. The fighting blood was quickly rekindled. There was an anxiousness in many of the warriors. Knowing that they would be leaving the valley before the day was gone, they wanted to finish these soldiers. And there was an avenging to be done, for all the good men lost yesterday.

The soldiers were quickly encircled. Some warriors moved in closer and closer, ducking in and out of cover, trying to decoy the soldiers into using up their bullets and jamming their guns. As those warriors baited the soldiers, many others were preparing for a charge. By now the sun was already high, but still on the morning side of its climb, and once again most of the warriors in the encampment had reached the fighting. They scattered themselves around the soldier barricade, and waited to engulf the tight knot of soldiers somehow still able to cling to their lives.

A shout signaled the first charge of the day. Horses already worked into their second wind thundered toward the soldier hill. Gunfire was a long, rolling noise. It was difficult for the warriors to see the damage they were causing since the soldiers were bunched together, most of them shoulder-to-shoulder. Some of the warriors rode close enough to see frightened, gray faces. But a few paid for their reckless daring. The charge veered off and settled into a high lope as warriors moved out of range of soldier guns. For a time there was no fire from the soldiers. But some of the warriors sitting in close could see movement. The soldiers were repositioning themselves inside their shelter.

Crazy Horse had reached the fighting, with Big Road of the Oglala and Black Moon of the Hunkpapa. He rode to the top of a hill far out of range of soldier guns. He had been told that some of the old men leaders were coming, too, to try to talk the warriors into breaking off the fight. The Oglala did not want to place the old warriors in danger, so he stayed on the hill and waited for the old men leaders to arrive. In the meantime, warriors closer to the barricade began to exchange a steady fire with the soldiers. Somewhere below the soldier hill, below the bluff on the riverside, there was more gunfire. Crazy Horse couldn't see them, but he knew that warriors were on the west-facing slopes, between the soldiers and the river. Perhaps they had charged the soldiers, too. It seemed so, from the sounds of the firing from the west end of the soldier position.

As word spread that Crazy Horse was on the field, some of the warrior leaders rode to his position. Most of them were in favor of over-running the soldiers with several charges, one wave of warriors after another. Others favored waiting them out. There was something to be said for both ways. Several hard charges would bring about the same end as yesterday on the hills further to the north. But that way could mean more good men getting hurt, and killed. Some had gone down already in the first charge. Keeping the soldiers hemmed-in behind their shelters and waiting them out would be easier. Thirst would get them, cut off from the river as they were. Hunger, too, eventually. Their wounded would all die, too. But reports of more soldiers further to the north could make waiting more dangerous for the Lakota and Cheyenne. That, and the old men leaders' advice to break off the fighting and move the people south, raised a need for urgency.

A tired warrior, about to wear out his fourth mount in two days of fighting, spoke up. "The soldiers left over there are beaten," he said. "They can do no more than wait for us to kill them. We have won. They know that. We know that. I agree with the old men. It is easier for us to die, than it is for our families to live with our deaths. We should not raise the price of victory so high. It is our women and children who must pay it."

Many around Crazy Horse sat for a time with eyes downcast. No one could argue with the wisdom of him who had spoken, especially since his reputation as a fighting man was strong.

"My friends," Crazy Horse said, after a long silence. "The

words we have heard are true. I, too, agree with the old men. But you know that it is not our way for one man to say, 'Do this, and do that.' Each man must decide for himself. We fought hard at Rosebud Creek. We fought hard here. And we have won each time. And if you want to keep fighting, I will ride with you. But I think we should stop when our families are packed and ready for travel. Even if the soldiers are still alive."

Every head in the circle of warriors around the Oglala nodded in agreement. Then some rode off to pass the word.

Below the bluffs, on a flat shelf as wide as a man is tall, two warriors peered over the edge of a gully's rim. Soldiers were being positioned in some of the narrow washes. Soldier leaders were plainly trying to extend and strengthen the soldier lines. White Feather Tail ducked below the gully's rim and cast a knowing glance toward his cousin. The soldiers could not be allowed to widen the area they could cover with their gunfire.

"It is time to use your bullets," he told his cousin.

But before Bear could take aim, someone else squeezed off a shot. In less than a heartbeat, the west-facing slope of the bluffs turned into a hot battlefield. Some of the soldiers were hit, and no soldier seemed willing to die to hold the new position. They scrambled back up the slope toward the barricade, perhaps realizing that the warrior force below the bluffs was stronger than they had thought. Many of the warriors took advantage of the brief soldier retreat to move up the slopes themselves, moving close so as to be within bow range. The advance brought them close enough that a short run would take them into the soldier barricade. For that kind of fighting, only the war club and lance would be needed. But for the time being, they only watched and waited, now and then getting off a fast shot at a soldier's head, and keeping all the bluecoats pinned down.

North and east of the bluffs, another mounted charge was forming. Warriors checked their rifles and revolvers and nervously looked at the distance to the soldier entrenchments. Suddenly, the charge was underway. Warriors on foot and hiding behind cover jumped up and followed the horsemen. Again, the warriors veered their sweep to the left and poured a continuous fire into the tight bunch of soldiers. Like before, it was difficult to know how much damage was done. But at least they had provided a covering fire for the warriors on foot to move closer. Once close enough, the silent, deadly bow was the best weapon. It did not give away the shooter's position with noise or a puff of telltale smoke.

Crazy Horse and the old men leaders, who had arrived in time to see the end of the second charge, watched and listened as the fighting wore on. Unlike those yesterday on the bottoms and on the hills north above the camp, these soldiers were showing a stubborn will to stay alive. They were dug-in and could defend themselves better from their position.

One of the old men leaders spoke as he cast wise and knowing eyes over the battlefield. "Yesterday soldiers attacked foolishly. Perhaps thinking they were stronger because they are bluecoats. Perhaps thinking we would be easy to defeat. Or perhaps not knowing that we can be strong. We should be careful not to think that way."

The man paused, then pointed a coup stick covered with many, many eagle feathers toward the soldiers. "They are defeated. Let them live, so they can face the shame of it every day for as long as they are alive. They have seen and felt the power that we carry as warriors. Let them live so they can tell of it to their own kind. That would be another kind of victory for us. And then, maybe they will stop being such a bothersome thing."

Warriors were gathering on the bottoms north of the bluffs to join those already up on the hills around the soldiers. The sun was high now, close to the top of its climb. Off to the north, buzzards were wheeling in broad circles, riding the high, hot breezes. So many dots against the pale sky. Some were over the soldier barricade, too. A hot breeze crawled over the bluffs, over the barricades. Carrying the stink of bloated flesh across the hills and into the gullies. It fluttered eagle feathers tied to lances and coup sticks. It twirled those tied to warrior hair, and then it calmed itself.

Gunfire fell away, with only a few shots cracking into the hot air above the hills. Crazy Horse had sent word. Warriors should hold themselves back for a time, and let the sun's heat fight the soldiers.

The sun climbed higher. As it reached the middle of the sky, gunfire came from the west, below the soldier barricade. Soldiers were going for water. A large group of them. Bullets and arrows filled the ravines and shrub patches along which the soldiers moved. Some were hit, their bodies raising dust when they fell. But a few did reach the water, hurriedly dipping kettles and cups before they dashed back across the open space for better cover. The hiss and snap of arrows were lost amidst the boom of rifles, and the dull crack of an occasional revolver being fired. Water was worth much to the soldiers this day, and they were paying the price. Here and there, one dashed in to pull or carry a fallen one to safety. It was good to see, in a way. Yesterday, in the retreat across the bottoms and through the timber, many soldiers had been left behind. It was good to see that at least one or two of them were worthwhile enemies this day. Some of the warriors eased up on their firing and let the soldiers scramble back over the bluff rim. They had very little water for their trouble, perhaps just enough to tease the thirst and sharpen it. Like the few sprinkles of rain felt during the night.

Two messengers found Crazy Horse and passed on word from Sitting Bull. Many of the lodges had been struck. The people would be ready to move before sundown. But the move must be done in the daylight so travel could be slow, to be careful with the wounded. One of the messengers lingered a little and moved his horse closer to the Oglala war leader.

"Uncle," he said in a low voice, "the dead ones across the

river are starting to stink. The smell sometimes reaches the camps."

After the messengers rode away, Crazy Horse motioned for Black Moon and Big Road. "If some could fire from the south and west long enough to keep the soldiers busy, others could try another charge. Then, we can leave. It is no use to waste any more time here."

A good man was sent to carry the message to the warriors on the slopes below the soldiers. The warriors to the north and east were told to hold for a time after the firing began from the bluffs. Then, there would be one last charge.

Sudden and fast gunfire came from below the bluff rim. It remained steady. Some of the warriors were surprised that those below the bluffs still had so many bullets. Return-fire from the soldiers was light, showing that they were pinned-down behind their positions. Then, from the north and east, mounted warriors charged from several different places. But many of them rode only a short hard gallop and dismounted, to move up on the soldiers under cover. They fired and moved to cover and then crawled to jump up from another place to fire again. The firing at the soldiers was continuous, though they returned fire at a good rate. But without much damage. Warriors were keeping themselves too well hidden.

And then a strange thing happened. A group of soldiers left the safety of the barricade and charged at some warriors closer in. Perhaps hot sun and thirst had driven them to craziness. But the pitiful charge did not last. Warriors to the left and right of the crazy ones drove them back easily.

Soon after that word was again passed to the warriors. It was time to leave. Time to go home to wives and children. The few warriors who had been hit had been retrieved. Then the warriors left. Because they could.

The sun was into the afternoon part of the sky as a strange silence came to the valley of the Greasy Grass. There was no more gunfire. The fevered blood of the warriors began to cool. As they returned to the camps, with most of the lodges already taken down, the sounds of children seemed to be the most easily heard, sounds which told that not all of the things which lay in a warrior's path were dangerous. And then the women began to trill, a sound that carried through the cottonwoods, moving like a cool breeze rippling a quiet stream. The sound of victory. One to quicken the heart, and to bring a tear to the corner of an eye in even the stoniest of faces.

Only a small handful of warriors stayed behind to watch the soldiers. And even that was not really a needed thing. In spite of the silence, the soldiers stayed behind the barricade.

There was an urgency in the camps. There were more reports of other soldier columns to the north and the horse herds had cropped down the grass further and further from the river. Two good reasons to hurry. The occasional smell of rotting flesh floating in on a wandering breeze hurried everyone a little, too.

Some families had to leave belongings behind. Sometimes all of a lodge's poles were left as people packed things considered more important. Or to have room to carry the wounded, and some of the dead, too, which would be placed on scaffolds nearer to the Shining Mountains. New lodge poles could be cut.

Except for the smallest children, everyone was busy. With most of the lodges down, the appearance of the encampment changed. The activity was the biggest change. People were busy with the chore of moving, instead of the usual everyday things of camp life. Only days before they had moved up from Ash Creek. Now they talked about the Shining Mountains as they worked. There was country pleasing to the eye. Good hunting. And no soldiers, dead or alive.

Sitting Bull moved among the activity. There were other changes, too. Changes not easily seen. Only felt, by those looking for such things. Three hard-fought battles in two days was no small thing, even for a warrior people. Death brought the biggest change to some of the lodges. A hunter and a warrior, a family's protector and provider, was the hardest and most frightening kind of loss. It was hard because the hunter and warrior was also a man, a husband, a father, son, grandson, and friend. It was frightening because the empty place at the back of the lodge was a dark hole in the tomorrows yet to come. That many, many more bluecoats had died was no consolation. One warrior, one man, one true human being lost dimmed any victory. And a memory could not hunt, or hold his children, or be a warmth beneath the sleeping robes. The price of victory had been high.

The Hunkpapa holy man could feel something welling up in his eyes as he walked and thought of those things. But he did not try to stop it, even as he heard a voice call to him. A tall warrior caught up with him, one whose warrior society had been picked by the old men leaders to ride guard during the move.

"Grandfather," the warrior called. "We are sending the young men to begin gathering up the horse herds. The old ones in the council lodge think it is time to send criers among the people, and to ask everyone to line up with their own camps."

Sitting Bull smiled and nodded. "Yes," he replied. "It is time."

Once again the earth shook from the thunderous sweep of thousands of horses. Even those who had seen similar sights paused long enough to watch, agreeing that they were watching the biggest herd ever gathered by the Lakota. A herd being moved and guided by two or three hundred young men and older boys.

And then the people began to move.

Horse hooves and drag poles raised billowing clouds of dust which rose high into the late afternoon sky. The column stretched out slowly until the moving mass covered a large part of the valley floor, with the great horse herd on its western edge. By the time the very last ones urged their travois horses into a slow walk, the horses at the front had already worked up a sweat. When all of the people were finally moving, the length of the column was greater than the length of the encampment before the lodges were struck.

The members of one of the warrior societies, given the honor and responsibility of guarding the people as they moved, rode on the outermost edges. Their horses were all painted alike and each warrior wore his finest, and carried the special weapons and objects showing him as one of those picked for the honor. It was an old, old way, going back far beyond the time of horses.

Other warriors rode at the edge of the column or somewhere within it, staying close to the people in their own camp circles. Lances pointed to the sky. Eagle feathers fluttered in the breeze.

There were smiles and laughter. Here and there, a few daring glances toward a young warrior with newly won honors. Or from such a warrior toward a girl whose smile brought sudden clumsiness to the feet and a stirring to the heart.

Some families traveled quietly, with a pain still too fresh to allow them easy unguarded smiles. Some carried the reason for their quietness on drag poles, wrapped in burial robes, to be buried in the sky somewhere in the Shining Mountains.

Some looked back toward the now lonely cottonwoods on the Greasy Grass Meadow. Others gazed toward the hills and gullies across the river, toward the places where soldiers died. They remembered stories of the fighting, of warriors recognizing some among the soldiers who had been friends to the Lakota. Like the black-skinned one, and the one through whose veins flowed some Lakota blood. But he had died as Long Hair's man. They talked of the vision given to their great holy man, and of how it had come to pass. They wondered what that would mean for the tomorrows still coming.

Slowly, they moved out of the valley of the Greasy Grass River, happy to be Lakota, and of the Earth. Thankful for their victories, and hoping that their road hereafter would be easier because of them. And far, far above the people and hidden by the dust cloud, two eagles slid through the sky in wide circles as the last red rays of daylight caught their wings. They rode the winds higher and higher until they faded into the tall sky.

Sintegaliska (Spotted Tail)
Photo courtesy of the Library of Congress.

The horse named "Comanche" was often touted as
"the only survivor of the Custer Massacre," and Regimental orders
specified that he was to be taken care of for the rest of his life.
This picture of him was taken by John C. H. Grabill and is dated 1887.
Photo: Courtesy of the Library of Congress.

CHAPTER 23

The Survivors

Sometime during the early morning hours on Tuesday, three days after the 7th Cavalry had gone so boldly into the valley of the Little Big Horn, four who had survived down in the brush guarding the river came up a coulee, and it was here that Lieutenant DeRudio stumbled over the dead body of an Indian. He pushed to his feet as Private O'Neil and the others came in from down-slope, DeRudio commenting, "Our luck still holds."

It had still held about this time yesterday morning, the sky tinged with false dawn, when Lieutenant DeRudio standing watch had seen a gray-horse troop trotting along the riverbank, led by a figure clad in buckskin and wearing a big, white hat. Believing it to be a cavalry detachment under Tom Custer, DeRudio had bolted out of hiding to shout a greeting across the river. In response there had come a hail of bullets to send DeRudio scampering back into the bushes.

What he'd glimpsed were Sioux warriors astride cavalry horses and clad in the spoils of war and intent on more urgent business than a lone soldier.

Even as Lieutenant DeRudio went ahead up the coulee, a rifle barked, and he said, "Sounded like a Henry." He knew the Sioux had left snipers behind, with DeRudio's fears now that one of the sentries he'd spotted up on the bluffs would open fire. He raised a warning hand to halt the others.

Then he shouted, "Hold your fire! It's Lieutenant DeRudio and three others!"

"DeRudio? We gave you up for dead."

"By rights we should be." He struggled the final few yards to come out onto the crest of a bluff. With a wide smile for a corporal and three others coming up, he added, "Thirty hours is a long time between meals."

"Reno'll sure be pleased to see you, sir."

Lieutenant Charles DeRudio held there as Trooper O'Neil and Jackson and Girard shuffled toward the new perimeter. He looked northerly to where the defensive stand had been made by Reno's battalion. From there came the stench of dead horses and mules, and he supposed a lot of men he knew had gone down. He couldn't believe that it was over, that he'd survived. He asked one of the troopers, "Does anybody know what has happened to the Regiment?"

"Major Reno is holding us here, as he fears the Sioux will be back."

"And nothing of Terry," DeRudio murmured inwardly as he turned and moved wearily toward the perimeter.

Inside the new perimeter Major Marcus Reno was renewing his orders that every man be ready to take to the pits in case there was an attack. For the horses, it was the first time since Saturday that saddles were removed, and accompanied by armed guards, troopers brought the horses down to the river for watering. Other orders were directed by Reno at Trumpeter Martin, to the effect he had sounded retreat, recall, and march, to draw in any command that might be concealed out there someplace. Through all of this

Reno was deaf to suggestions from other officers that a patrol be sent up north to scout out the Regiment's last known position. Strangely, Captain Benteen, now that the immediate danger was over, was keeping his distance from Reno and any thoughts of command.

Benteen was one of the first to greet DeRudio and his comrades, the welcome news spreading quickly, while the sky was brightening quickly. And as the sun began climbing away from the horizon, those who'd fought Indians before were beginning to realize that the Sioux might be gone for good.

And they had no way of knowing that just to the north about four miles the Montana column as coming in.

* * * * * * *

Crow scout Curly was out front with those taking in the blackened prairie smoldering under a sooty haze up-valley where the great Sioux encampment had so recently stood. He nudged his pony after the officers swirling about General Terry, there to have Terry lay somber eyes upon the young Crow.

"Up by those bluffs is where you last saw Custer ...?" General Terry asked him.

Curly nodded.

"I have a patrol heading there now," said the General. But this village ... the largest I've ever seen."

Down toward the river the column wended, to find a crossing and surge across the Greasy Grass. Orders were given to have the first company fan-out and search through the litter and debris, and there were the carcasses of ponies. Standing among this were two funeral lodges. The General was brought over to view the heads of three soldiers placed near the top of a lodgepole. The heads had been scalped and burned, and battered beyond recognition. Other evidence of what Terry feared most was the finding of mutilated bodies, items of army clothing.

"Here, sir, this bullet-riddled buckskin shirt. It belonged to Lieutenant Porter."

And then a blood-soaked pair of drawers marked "Sturgis - Seventh Cavalry" brought home the horrible truth to everyone there. Then came the shout that the patrol was coming in from the bluffs.

Curly hung back some as the officer in charge of the patrol gave his report that he'd found the bodies of about two-hundred men spread out amongst the bluffs and ravines.

"No survivors."

"Custer ?"

"We did not go in that close, sir. But from the looks of the bodies, and the way the horses are bloated, it happened a couple of days ago."

Curly brought his horse in closer, to draw attention to him and where he was pointing. One of the officers produced a field glass, scoped-in on three riders skylined along the bluffs to the south. "They're troopers, sir — must be from Reno's battalion."

From all that Curly had told him, General Alfred Terry knew that Reno was still in the dark as to the fate of George Custer. "We'll have to get word to Reno. Curly, if you'll go along."

The same patrol that had found the bodies of Custer and his command cut just to the north and to where Medicine Tail Coulee ventured down to the river. As he rode, Curly slowed up to take a lingering look back at General Terry. He saw tears touching upon the general's cheeks, and he realized this man was mourning the passing of Yellow Hair. What had the horse soldiers called it? Yes, they had spoken of Custer's luck.

"No more," Curly thought to himself, "as it has been stolen by Sitting Bull's vision of a great victory."

Now reining onward, he passed through cottonwoods throwing down cottony seeds that billowed about Curly heading his horse across the Greasy Grass and after the horse soldiers striking up the coulee.

"Sunrise on Custer's Battlefield,"
courtesy of the Denver Public Library,
photograph by Richard Throssel, 1911,
Call Number: X-31533.

Captain (formerly Lieutenant) DeRudio, 7th Cavalry,
courtesy of the Denver Public Library,
Photo by D. F. Barry, 1879,
Call Number: B-52.

Epilogue

The road to the Agency town was long and dusty. It was hot so they stopped several times to rest the horses and sit in the shade under the wagon. When the Agency, with its squat brick buildings and an assortment of other drab structures came into view, there was no sense of relief for the end of a long journey. With narrowed eyes, chiseled into the bronzed and sunburnt face, the man on the wagon seat surveyed the settlement. Life a wolf venturing into unknown territory, or a warrior scouting enemy country. A boy beside the deep-chested, heavily-muscled man looked about with eight-year-old curiosity.

Could this be the place where the Pawnees were caught sneaking into Lakota country, the man wondered. From where they had been chased down into the sand hills country, and killed to a man?

This place did not have the look or feel of victory. It was a place of blowing sand, tumbleweeds, and square houses with dark doorways. It was the Agency. A place where the whites sat and issued meat, flour, coffee, and orders. Someplace to be avoided, if at all possible.

He could not avoid coming here any longer. It was finally out of concern for his wife and son that he was here. He was here to touch the paper. To take a piece of Earth marked out for him. One-hundred sixty acres, since he had a family.

The sun was well into the afternoon sky when he was finally called into a room. A tall, bewhiskered man with a French name carefully explained to him in Lakota about the land. He kept the boy close and endured the explanation. Suddenly, the Frenchman was standing before him with a bow and one arrow, calling for him to follow. Bewildered, the man stood and grabbed the boy's hand.

He was led outside and into a dusty field with a gentle upslope. They stopped beside a single-bottom plow squatting in the dust. Now he knew that things he had heard were true. He knew what was expected of him. For a moment he considered refusing. But that would not be good. He was here for his wife and son. Not for himself.

Before the bearded man was finished with his instructions, the dark-faced man held out his hands for the bow and arrow. There had been knowing or suspicious glances, over the years, from such as this Agency man. He knew they suspected him of being at the Greasy Grass Fight. One or two of his own relatives had asked him about it. But since that day, now twenty winters past, he had not spoken of it.

The man, dressed in rumpled, baggy wool trousers and a faded calico shirt, took the bow and arrow. Trying to appear clumsy, he nocked the arrow to the string and stared off into the distance. And to a place in time. At first the sounds and images in his memory were faint. But they grew stronger. Confused soldiers. Screaming horses. The smell of blood and burning grass. And the three-arrows game.

With smooth, unforgotten motion, he drew the bow. Pushing and pulling at the same time, he angled the shot into the sky and the arrow flew in a smooth and gentle arc. It impaled the Earth with a puff of dust.

He gave the bow back to the Frenchman, and took two steps toward the jutting handles of the plow. His strong, dark hands wrapped around the shiny wood, for a heartbeat or two.

Let them think I might be a farmer, he said to himself. He took the boy's hand again and hurried back inside the brick building. Hurrying to touch the paper for the land. For his son. But he kept his head high, so the boy could not see the tears sliding down the dark face.

"Sunrise on Custer Battle field, the Custer scouts are
Indians who were with Custer on the morning of the fight,"
courtesy of the Denver Public Library,
photograph by Richard Throssel, 1908,
Call Number: X-31546.

Afterword

I. THE CAVALRY

The 1876 expedition was to be in the words of the Department of the Army the greatest military action ever undertaken by the government against the Indians of the Great Plains. The tri-pronged plan involved Army columns heading out of Forts Fetterman, Ellis, and Abraham Lincoln, then to converge upon the suspected location of the Indians someplace east and north of the Big Horn Mountains. Mostly it was an army of raw recruits sprinkled with veterans of the Civil War and the Indians Wars. It was also an army commanded by three men holding Presidential ambitions, Crook, Gibbon, and George Armstrong Custer.

II. THE MEN

GEORGE ARMSTRONG CUSTER, LIEUTENANT COLONEL, 36. His family called him Autie. There was another nickname, that of "Old Curly," which had been affectionately bestowed by the men in the ranks under him. He was a slender five feet seven inches tall. There was the tawny mustache, the deeply-set clear blue eyes, the long, gold-tinted hair. There was the court-martial ordered by General Grant at Fort Leavenworth, Kansas. A guilty verdict saw the Boy General suspended from rank and command for one year, and he felt his reputation tarnished.

Reinstated a year later at the request of Generals, Sherman, Sully, and Sheridan, he resumed command of his beloved 7th Cavalry. As for the men he commanded, there were no middle-of-the-road feelings, for they were either intensely loyal or sullen and secretly insubordinate. Other troubles cropped up for the Boy General after he was ordered to Fort Abraham Lincoln, this in the form of charges he brought against Secretary of War W. W. Belknap, in that Belknap was profiteering in the revenues of traders at Army posts.

At the time he was summoned to Washington, D.C., to testify at Congressional hearings, his regiment was preparing for a spring campaign against the Indians. While there he was told that President Grant had ordered another officer be placed in command of the Seventh Cavalry. He fled Washington, only to be arrested when he entrained in Chicago, but was allowed to go onto St. Paul to plead his case before General Alfred Terry. Which he did, on bended knee. Much to his joy a telegram sent by Terry to the White House saw Grant relent.

And back at Fort Abraham Lincoln, the Boy General knew the seeds he had sown through the *New York Herald* could possibly see him nominated as the Democratic candidate in this Presidential election year. But there was the need to remove the tarnish from his name in a glorious victory over the mighty Sioux Nation.

MARCUS A. RENO, MAJOR. Custer's second in command. He was known to the Indian scouts attached to the Seventh Cavalry as "The Man With Dark Face." And like Custer, he had distinguished himself in the Civil War. Ironically, he had been on the board which approved the Springfield rifle, the principal weapon of the troops at the Little Big Horn. In that battle, Springfields captured from the soldiers fighting under George Custer's direct command were turned upon Reno and his three companies.

In frequent bouts with the bottle, he drank to excess and became embittered and withdrawn, his self-confidence gradually eroding. And some felt that he was incapable of command on June 25, 1876. Reno's rash nature saw him making a presumptuous bid for power. This in the late spring of 1876, when he attempted to wrest command of the 7th cavalry from General Custer. After his commander had been summoned to Washington, D.C., he wired General Terry asking for a chance to take over the regiment. Even before this he had associated himself with the anti-Custer faction within the regiment.

FREDERICK W. BENTEEN, CAPTAIN. Cool-headed, Brave, Vindictive. His bright, ruddy pleasant face framed by snowy hair, he would sit around a campfire at night with men of lesser rank, beaming with kindness and humor, even though there were dark secrets lurking behind his round, cynical eyes.

An anonymous letter he wrote to a Missouri friend soon appeared in the *Missouri Democrat,* the contents of which cast a pall of doubt upon the outcome of the Washita fight.

This battle had been chronicled by the military as a brilliant and well-executed conquest over the Indians. The letter, to which he professed authorship in a bitter argument with Custer, accused the adored Boy General as being worthy of court-martial for what Benteen called unjustifiably deserting Major Elliot and his men, killed by the Cheyenne, with their bodies horribly mutilated. He never apologized. The rift continued to deepen between the two men.

CURLY, CROW SCOUT, 17. Darkly handsome and tall, as

were many Crow, he was in the vanguard of Arikara and Crow scouts scouting southwesterly through the valley of the Rosebud. The signs they found were plentiful, ominous, not one trail but a wide track gouging into the valley floor and touching the foothills to either side. A track made by hundreds of Sioux Indians and their allies, a horse herd numbering in the thousands.

Through the sudden clutch of fear, there was also the secret Curly shared with the other Crow scouts. For they alone knew word had been leaked to Sitting Bull and the Sioux that many soldiers were coming. He had learned to be loyal to the soldiers only in that, as told to him by his elders and the chiefs, it would mean survival for the Crow Nation.

This was another mystery he kept locked inside, but puzzled over, for the Sioux and Crow had always been mortal enemies. He must seek a deeper meaning from this, but first there was this night and the dangers lurking ahead.

CRAZY HORSE. Crazy Horse, the Oglala, was perhaps the single most influential war leader of the Lakota (or western Sioux). His leadership was the deciding factor in the Battle of the Rosebud. And the defeat of General George Crook at the Rosebud was the forerunner for victory eight days later at the Battle of the Little Big Horn.

Crazy Horse's influence was largely by example, but because of that his word also carried weight. He understood that if the Lakota were to have any chance of permanently pushing the white man out of their lands, the Lakota attitude toward how to go about fighting them would need to change. In a council shortly before the Battle of the Rose bud, he convinced his fellow warriors to fight a war of attrition against the whites.

The extent of Crazy Horse's influence is evident in that his fellow warriors took his word to heart. About a thousand of them followed him into battle against Crook. Crook, with a force of about 1,500 — including about 200 Crow and Shoshone Indians —

did manage to avoid being completely overrun. Still, his losses were heavier than those of the Lakota and Cheyenne. Though he claimed victory, General Crook was unable to put an effective fighting unit into the field for many weeks afterward .

Crook's defeat added to the power and influence of Crazy Horse. Some historians think that the Battle of the Rosebud is his finest military triumph. But, of course, the Oglala war leader did not think in those terms. His main concern was for his people, their very lives as well as their way of life. That was typical of the man.

He was not given to wearing or displaying the decorative symbols of the many war honors he had earned, as was the custom for Lakota warriors. He was shy about recounting his deeds in battle, though that too was a customary thing for warriors to do. It was this characteristic which helped to endear him to the people, and earn him the label of "Our Strange Man." For it was strange, indeed, for a formidable Lakota warrior not to talk about his exploits. Even with his own family.

His achievements as a warrior were many. In 1866, ten years before the Battle of the Rosebud and the Little Big Horn, he led a group of warriors to decoy a detachment from Fort Philip Kearney, on the banks of the Little Piney near the Bozeman Trail, out into the open and into a pitched battle with hidden Lakota and Cheyenne warriors. White historians call it "The Fetterman Massacre." It was a hard-fought engagement. Crazy Horse and his small group of decoys were successful in luring an overconfident cavalry commander into the field. It was exploits like that which won him many honors as a young warrior. It was said of Crazy Horse that by his late teens, he had accumulated more honors than many warriors did in an entire lifetime. Because of his achievements and a genuine concern for the welfare of his people, he was asked to take positions of leadership.

Some writers of the history of the High Plains have called him a blood-thirsty savage and the son of a white man. He was neither of these. He was, however, the epitome of a Lakota warrior. Courageous in battle and generous to his people.

At the Battle of the Rosebud and the Little Big Horn, his influence, from a quiet man who led by example, was perhaps the most formidable enemy that Crook and Custer could have faced. They certainly did see and experience the manifestation of that influence. It rode with the Lakota and Cheyenne warriors as they handed the United States Army the two worst defeats of the Indian/White Wars of the High Plains.

SITTING BULL. In the summer of 1876, two men among the Lakota (Western Sioux) were at the pinnacle of their power and influence: Crazy Horse and Sitting Bull.

Sitting bull was a Hunkpapa Lakota and Crazy Horse Ogala Lakota. The Hunkpapa was the older of the two.

In the spring of 1876, Sitting Bull sent out the word for a gathering near the Shining Mountains (Big Horns). That area, along with Bear Butte (in what is now South Dakota) was a favorite place for such things. The summer of 1876 was by no means the first gathering of the Lakota to have taken place near the Greasy Grass River (known to the whites as Little Big Horn). Because of his reputation and status among the Lakota, and because of the growing concern over the problem of white encroachment into Lakota territory, the people came from all parts of the nation. In addition to Sitting Bull's call, some of the Oglala bands had selected Crazy Horse as their overall leader. That was additional incentive for people to come together. But it was to Sitting Bull and his power and influence as a medicine-man that the Lakota initially responded. At the time of the U.S. Seventh Cavalry's attack on the great encampment on the Greasy Grass, the people in the camps numbered as many as ten-thousand men, women, and children. Included were a small number of Northern Cheyenne.

Early in June, some days before the Rosebud Battle of the 17th,

Sitting Bull participated in the Sun Dance and came away with the prophecy of a great victory over soldiers. He had a vision of "many soldiers falling into camp." The vision served as inspiration for the warriors who fought General George Crook's numerically superior force to a standstill on the Rosebud Creek. But, as the Lakota were to realize only eight days later, that battle was not the focus of Sitting Bull's vision. The vision came to pass on the 25th day of June when the Seventh Cavalry attacked the great encampment on the banks of the Greasy Grass River.

In some ways Sitting Bull was an enigma. Years after the Battle of the Greasy Grass (or the Little Big Horn), when he saw that its consequences were largely disastrous for the Lakota, he fled to Grandmother's Land — Canada — with some of his people. He returned in 1881 and later traveled and performed with Buffalo Bill Cody's Wild West Show. After that, when the Ghost Dance phenomena swept through the High Plains, he participated. The Ghost Dancers believed that their dancing would bring back the old Lakota way of life and drive the white man away. It was a concept which the Hunkpapa medicine-man strongly favored. But because Sitting Bull still wielded much influence among the Lakota in 1890, the United States Government was fearful that his participation in the Ghost Dance would instigate a general uprising.

In December of 1890 the government sent a contingent of Indian police, considered by them to be progressive Indians, to arrest Sitting Bull at his camp near the Grand River. The medicine-man resisted and was killed. (Two weeks later, elements of the U.S. Seventh and Ninth Cavalries caught up with Big Foot's band of Miniconju Lakota and escorted them to Wounded Knee Creek on the Pine Ridge Reservation.)

Sitting Bull, the Hunkpapa, was a warrior and a medicine-man. His exploits as a warrior and his power as a medicine-man brought him status and a position of leadership among the Lakota. Some historians, uninformed about the structure of Lakota society, speculate that he had planned the Battles of the Rosebud and the Little Big Horn. In reality, what he did was greater than that. He inspired Lakota and Cheyenne warriors to fight, to draw on a lifetime of training and to bring it to bear in defense of their people and their way of life. That is the true legacy of Sitting Bull.

WHITE FEATHER TAIL AND KILLS IN WATER. Two of the 800 to 2,000 warriors in the camp on the banks of the Little Big Horn were White Feather Tail and Kills In Water. They were Sicangu, but they were not the only Sicangu warriors present.

The Sicangu, or *burnt thigh,* were also called Brule by the French, and known today as the Rosebud Sioux. White Feather Tail and Kills In Water were first-cousins, both about seventeen or eighteen years of age. Before the battle, Kills In Water was known as Bear.

The two young men had traveled to the great encampment from the Spotted Tail Agency, some three-hundred miles to the southeast. Lured by news of Crazy Horse and harboring an intense distaste for the sedentary "do-nothing" life at Spotted Tail, they borrowed a horse each and rode west to join the Oglala war leader. Both young men were nearly six feet tall. White Feather Tail was stocky, and Bear was slender and quick. They were also quiet and reserved.

Their only possessions were two changes of clothes each and weapons. Bear had a decrepit breech-loading rifle and a few rounds of ammunition. They both had bows and arrows, and replenished their supplies of arrows on the trip west.

They were not only related, they were also the best of friends. And their hopes and dreams took them west toward the Shining Mountains to join others who would follow Crazy Horse.

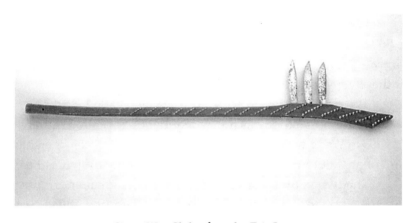

Sioux War Club, photo by Eric Long.
Wooden club decorated with brass tacks, with government-issued
knives attached. This War Club belonged to Chief Spotted Eagle, who
fought at the Little Bighorn. It is from the Keppler Collection.
Photo courtesy of The Smithsonian Institution.

The Number of Warriors and Their Armament

Since the battle of the Little Big Horn, white historians and writers have tendered many estimates regarding the number of warriors who took part in the Battle and the extent of their armament. Those estimates do vary, from as high as six-thousand to as low as one-thousand. The main justification for the high number seems to be that the only way the U.S. Cavalry could be defeated was by vastly superior numbers.

There were probably ten-thousand people — men, women, and children — encamped on the Little Big Horn. Included in that were a small number of Cheyenne. The exact number of full-fledged Lakota and Cheyenne warriors will never be known. But according to information passed down by some Lakota participants (to relatives or to other Indians and not to white interviewers), the usual historical estimate of five to six thousand warriors is excessive.

There were certainly between 4,000 and 6,000 *males* in the camp. However, the largest percentage would have been: (1) boys too young or not yet accomplished enough to take to the field as full-fledged warriors, and (2) old men past physical prime. With few exceptions, only full-fledged, physically able warriors took to the field. The Battle of the Little Big Horn might have been one of those few exceptions. But boys and old warriors certainly did not swell the warrior ranks to give the Lakota and Cheyenne the 10-to-1 advantage that is often bandied about.

Given the size of the two-generation Lakota and Cheyenne families during the era of the Battle, about eight members, some-where between 800 to 2,000 full-fledged warriors is a plausible estimate (notwithstanding the white eyewitnesses' penchant for inflating the numbers of opposing Indian warriors). But perhaps a more workable number is around 1,200.

Furthermore, it is probable that not all of the available warriors were able to take an active role in each segment of the Battle. This simply means that not all warriors engaged Reno on the bottoms. Likewise, not all available warriors engaged Custer.

Reno initially faced three-hundred to four-hundred warriors, and eventually as many as six-hundred. And most of the warriors did finally arrive at the site of Custer's demise, but many of them only after the fighting was over since they were intensely involved in pursuing Reno. It was not until the following morning , the 26th, that Reno and Benteen were finally faced with the largest warrior contingent: at least 1,000 warriors.

Eight-hundred to two-thousand against six-hundred is obviously a numerically superior force. But it important to note that not all of the warriors entered the fighting equipped with firearms. A significant number were armed with the bow and an average of 40 war arrows. Of course, a number could have picked up soldier rifles as the fighting progressed. Nevertheless, some among those with firearms had to eventually resort to the bow after expending their meager supplies of ammunition.

The Seventh Cavalry was outnumbered, but they were initially better-armed in terms of the long-range effectiveness of their rifles and the number of rounds of ammunition per man.

These more than merely plausible probabilities leave us with an interesting, largely overlooked, or purposely ignored fact: that the Seventh was simply outfought. Custer may have overestimated the fighting abilities of his troops, but he most certainly underestimated the ability of the Lakota warrior. Custer could not know, or begin to understand, that a Lakota warrior was not defined by the effectiveness or lack thereof of his weapons. There was more to *being* a Lakota warrior than weaponry. That aspect was not visible to Custer and his soldiers on that hot and dusty day in 1876. The invisible factor was the Lakota warrior's commitment to defend the people.

Given factors extant on June 25, 1876—numbers of opposing forces, types and extent of armament of opposing forces, the division of the invading force, weapon loss of the invading force and consequent weapon acquisition by the defending force—the Seventh Cavalry was doomed to defeat. But there is one more factor which is overlooked. It was that invisible factor of the Lakota warrior's commitment to defend the people.

The Seventh Cavalry carried a threat to the very edge of the great encampment on the banks of the Little Big Horn. In the camps were much that was held dear and sacred. The nature and proximity of the threat quickly brought that warrior commitment to the top. And it was that commitment, more than any other factor, which defeated the invader.

Biographies of Authors

Frederick Voget Lefthand

Frederick Voget Lefthand was born on the Crow Indian Reservation on April 7, 1943. His Christian name was given to him by Dr. Fred W. Voget, noted anthropologist and writer. Fred's father was a close friend and interpreter for Dr. Voget, who was living on the Crow Reservation at that time. Christian names, like Crow Indian names, are well thought out and have special meaning. Lefthand's family hoped that the name would bring their child recognition in education and security for the future.

All Crow Indians also have Indian names, names that they are known by among the tribe. Lefthand has five names, given at different intervals denoting personal achievements in education, public service, and the military. "High Bald Eagle" is the name by which he is known among the Crows at the present time.

After graduation from Lodge Grass High School, Lefthand enrolled at Bacone College. His college plans were interrupted by a tour of duty in Vietnam. After his honorable discharge, he enrolled at Rocky mountain College and received a B.S. in Economics and Business Administration in 1970.

Lefthand was elected Secretary of the Crow Tribal Council in 1970 at the age of 27. He served two terms in this capacity. Under the Crow form of government, the Secretary has equal veto power as the Chairman.

Orphaned at age 11, he was raised by his oldest brother, Ira Lefthand, who made sure Frederick learned the important culture and traditions of the Crow tribe. Lefthand was taught early the matrilineal system of the Clans and understood his responsibilities as a member of the Big lodge and a child of the Whistling Water Clans. Taught by clan elders, Lefthand understands the respect system involving all forms of life as well as the cosmos. One of his earliest teachers was Jack Little Nest, a well known story-teller among the

Crows. Little Nest, owner of a powerful medicine bundle, still among the Crows today, has shared his version of the Battle at the Little Big Horn.

Jack Little Nest's grandfather was the father-in-law of Mitch Bouyer, the half-breed scout who died in the Battle.

White Man Runs Him was one of Custer's Crow scouts, and is a relative of Fred Lefthand.

Lefthand's great grandfather was an Oglala Sioux. His name was Bird Tail That Rattles. Captured by the Crows at the age of six, he grew up to be a Crow warrior. He fought the Sioux more than once. Lefthand identifies with the fearsome band of Oglala Sioux headed by Chief Crazy Horse, sometimes referred to as the Iooxpa (The Men). Bird Tail That Rattles' warrior deeds and warrior songs are still kept by the Lefthand family.

While many accounts of the Battle of the Little Big Horn have been recorded and conclusions drawn over the past 130 years, little has been told by the tribes involved. Joe Marshall, noted Rosebud Sioux historian, Robert Kammen, a Western author, and Fred Lefthand have collaborated to share their point of view about what did happen at the Battle of the Little Big Horn. It is their purpose to give honor and recognition to the victories in their defense of their lands, people and way of life.

Fred Lefthand has served as Coordinator of Adult Education and an adjunct faculty member at Little Big Horn College in Crow Agency, Montana. He is married and has eight children and three grandchildren. He lives with his family on a ranch south of Lodge Grass at the foot of the Big Horn Mountains.

Joseph Marshall, III

Joseph Marshall, III, was born on the Rosebud Sioux Indian Reservation. Raised by maternal grandparents, his primary language since childhood is Lakota. English is his second language.

His childhood environment was filled with stories of his ancestors, and family ancestry in particular. His family is predominantly Sicangu, with some Oglala lineage from his paternal grand-father. It was his maternal grandfather, however, who was the main teacher and greatest influence in the formative years of boyhood. From him, young Joseph learned about the Lakota hunter-warrior traditions, even as he learned to make primitive Lakota bows and arrows. He was told about Lakota battles with the U.S. Cavalry, such as the Battle of the Greasy Grass River, long before he read about them in school. Of course, the versions he was taught in school were invariable different than those passed down through the ageless process of oral tradition.

Because of his grandparents' influence, Joseph has a deep, abiding interest in Native American history in general, and of the history of the Lakota in particular. He has developed and taught Lakota language courses at the high school and college levels, and has lectured on the Hunter-Warrior Traditions of the High Plains. Recently he served as a technical advisor for a television movie about the Lakota. Currently he is a Native American Studies con-sultant and teacher for Central Wyoming College. He takes special pride in having the knowledge and skill to hand craft authentic, primitive Lakota bows and arrows. Thanks to his grandfather.

Mr. Marshall is the father of six, ranging in age from twenty-two to one year; Kira, Michael, William, Erin, Steven, and Caitlin. Three daughters and three sons.

Mr. Marshall's Lakota name is Ohitiya Otanin, loosely translated as *His Courage Is Known.*

Robert Kammen

Over the years I have researched many parts of our American West. Out of this extensive research has come Western books pub-lished by Random House and others. I have found that part of this research brought me visiting on many occasions the Custer Battlefield up near Hardin, Montana, and on land that is still part of the Crow Indian Reservation.

Many books have been written about what happened here

back in June of 1876. Though every book I've read about this historic event was written by a white man. And like so many I accepted as fact much of what had been placed on paper. That is, until I was introduced to Wyomingite Dick Redland.

Though still a rancher, Mr. Redland now spends his winters down in Texas. But it was before his departure last fall that he and I got together, where I learned that Dick Redland had owned a ranch up near Lodge Grass, Montana. The talk got around to digs being conducted up at the Custer Battlefield, that in Mr. Redland's opinion much of what had been printed about the events of a century ago were erroneous. So it was that Dick Redland pointed me to the Crow Agency headquarters up near Hardin, where a friend of his was a professor of economics at the Crow College.

This turned out to be Freddie Lefthand, a Crow historian and fellow rancher. First of all, I learned from Mr. Lefthand that no book had ever been published by either the Crow or Teton Lakota telling the victor's side of the Lakota victory over the United States Army. After hearing Freddie Lefthand's version of what happened, I looked up Joe Marshall, a Brule Sioux (Sicangu Lakota) who had made a study of the Battle at Little Big Horn. Neither man having met before, it was very exciting to find the details they narrated to me of that battle were a carbon copy of one another.

I must point out that there was a time when the Crow and the Sioux were blood-enemies. But both Freddie Lefthand and Joe Marshall believe it is time the truth be told, a truth which they also believe will bring honor to both the Crow and the Teton Lakota.

One of the exciting things was of Freddie Lefthand taking me on a tour of the battlefield. He pointed out many inaccuracies that he had found in books, of distance, terrain, the route actually taken by George Armstrong Custer through the valley of the Little Big Horn and down to the Greasy Grass River. I will leave it here, to let the reader share in this book what we believe to be the truth as handed down from generation to generation by both the Crow and Teton Lakota.

Robert Kammen

259

References

Ambrose, Stephen E., *Crazy Horse & Custer: The Parallel Lives of Two American Warriors.* New York: Doubleday, 1975.

Andrist, Ralph K., *The Long Death: The Last Days of the Plains Indian.* New York: Collier Books, Macmillan Publishing Company, 1964.

Bachrach, Deborah, *Custer's Last Stand: Opposing Viewpoints.* San Diego, CA: Greenhaven Press, 1990.

Bear, Isaac, (1883 - 1954), Sicangu Lakota. Oral histories and recollections.

Black Elk. *Black Elk Speaks: Being the Life Story of a Holy Man of the Ogalala Sioux as told to John G. Niehardt.* New York: William Morrow & Co., 1932.

Brininstool, Earl Alonzo (1870 – 1957), *A Trooper with Custer & Other Historic Incidents of the Battle of the Little Big Horn.* Columbus, OH: The Hunter-Trader-Trapper Co., 1926.

Brown, Jesse; & A. M. Willard, *The Black Hills Trails: A History of the Struggles of the Pioneers in the Winning of the Black Hills.* Rapid City, SD: Rapid City Journal Co., 1924.

Camp, Walter Mason. *Custer in '76: Walter Camp's Notes on the Custer Fight.* Edited by Kenneth Hammer. Provo: Brigham Young University Press, 1976.

Connell, Evan S., *Son of the Morning Star.* San Francisco: North Point Press, 1984.

Dippie, Brian W. *Custer's Last Stand: The Anatomy of an American Myth.* Lincoln: University of Nebraska Press, 1976.

Dixon, Joseph Kossuth, *The Vanishing Race: The Last Great Indian Council.* New York: Doubleday, Page, & Co., 1913.

Ege, Robert J., *Curse Not His Curls.* Fort Collins, CO: The Old Army Press, 1974.

Fougera, Katherine Gibson, *With Custer's Cavalry.* Caldwell, ID: The Caxton Printers, Ltd., 1940.

Fox, Richard Allan, Jr. *Archaeology, History, and Custer's Last Battle: The Little Big Horn Reexamined.* Norman: University of Oklahoma Press, 1993.

Godfrey, Edward Settle (1843 – 1932), *Custer's Last Battle.* Golden, CO: Outbooks, 1986.

Godfrey, Edward Settle, *An Account of Custer's Last Campaign & the Battle of the Little Big Horn.* Palo Alto, CA: L. Osborne, 1968.

Graham, William Alexander (1875 – 1954), Colonel (Ret.). *Abstract of the Official Record of Proceedings of The Reno Court of Inquiry: Convened at Chicago, Illinois, 13 January, 1879.* Harrisburg: The Stack Pole Company, 1954. (Written in 1921.)

Graham, William Alexander, *The Custer Myth: A Source Book of Custeriana to Which Is Added Important Items of Custeriana & a Complete & Comprehensive Bibliography by Fred Dustin*. New York: Bonanza Books, 1953.

Graham, William Alexander, *Major Reno Vindicated*. Hollywood, CA: Privately published by E. A. Brininstool, 1935.

Graham, William Alexander, *The Story of the Little Big Horn: Custer's Last Fight*. New York: The Century Co., 1926.

Gray, John Stephens, *Custer's Last Campaign: Mitch Boyer & the Little Bighorn Reconstructed*. Lincoln: U. of Nebraska Press, 1991.

Greene, Jerome A., ed. *Battles and Skirmishes of the Great Sioux War, 1876-1877: The Military View*. Norman: University of Oklahoma Press, 1993.

Hardoff, Richard G., *Lakota Recollections of the Custer Fight: New Sources of Indian – Military History*. Spokane, WA: A. H. Clark Co., 1991.

Hatch, Thom. *Custer and the Battle of the Little Bighorn: An Encyclopedia of the People, Places, Events, Indian Culture and Customs, Information Sources, Art and Films*. Jefferson, NC: McFarland & Company, Inc., Publishers, 1997.

Hirst, Adrian E., *Custer's Wolves & Custer's Ifs*. Billings, MT: A. E. Hirst, 2004.

Hutton, Paul Andrew, ed. *The Custer Reader*. Lincoln: University of Nebraska Press, 1992.

Luce, Edward Smith, Captain, *Keogh, Commanche, & Custer*. Dedham, MA: E. S. Luce, 1939.

Marquis, Thomas Bailey (1869 – 1935), *Custer on the Little Bighorn: Eye Witness & Carefully Researched Accounts of Custer's Famous "Last Stand" Battle with the Cheyenne & Sioux Indians on June 25, 1876*. Lodi, CA: Dr. Marquis Custer Publications, 1967.

Marquis, Thomas Bailey, *Keep the Last Bullet for Yourself: The True Story of Custer's Last Stand*. New York: Two Continents Publishing Group, 1976.

Masters, Joseph G., *Shadows Fall Across the Little Big Horn: "Custer's Last Stand."* Laramie: U. of Wyoming Library, 1951.

Michno, Gregory, *The Mystery of E Troop: Custer's Gray Horse Company at the Little Bighorn*. Missoula, MT: Mountain Pass Publishing Co., 1994.

Miller, David Humphreys. *Custer's Fall: The Indian Side of the Story*. Lincoln: University of Nebraska Press, 1957.

Rankin, Charles E., ed. *Legacy: New Perspectives on the Battle of the Little Bighorn*. Helena: Montana Historical Society Press, 1996.

Reedstrom, Ernest Lisle, *Custer's 7th Cavalry: From Fort Riley to the Little Bighorn*. New York: Stirling Publishing Co., 1992.

Reusswig, William, *A Picture Report of the Custer Fight*. New York: Hastings House, 1967.

Robertson, William Glenn, Dr.; Dr. Jerold E. Brown; Major (Ret.) William M. Campsey; & Major (Ret.) Scott R. McMeen, *Atlas of the Sioux Wars.* Fort Leavenworth, Kansas: Combat Studies Institute, n.d.

Roe, Charles Frances (1848 – 1922), *Custer's Last Battle on the Little Big Horn, Montana Territory, June 25, 1876.* New York: Robert Bruce, 1927.

Sandoz, Mari, *The Battle of the Little Big Horn.* Philadelphia: J.B. Lippincott Company, 1966.

Sandoz, Mari, *Crazy Horse: The Strange Man of the Oglalas.* Lincoln: University of Nebraska Press, 1961.

Scott, Douglas D.; & Richard A. Fox Jr., *Archaeological Insights into the Custer Battle: An Assessment of the 1984 Field Season*, 1st edition. Norman: University of Oklahoma Press, 1987.

Scott, Douglass D.; Richard A. Fox Jr.; Melissa A. Connor; & Dick Harmon, *Archaeological Perspectives on the Battle of the Little Bighorn*, 1st edition. Norman: University of Oklahoma Press, 1989.

Scott, Douglas D.; Willey, P.; & Melissa A. Connor, *They Died with Custer: Soldiers' Bones from the Battle of the Little Bighorn.* Norman: University of Oklahoma Press, 1998.

Skelnar, Larry, *To Hell with Honor: Custer & the Little Bighorn.* Norman: University of Oklahoma Press, 2000.

Stewart, Edgar I., *Custer's Luck.* Norman: University of Oklahoma Press, 6th printing: 1971, originally 1955.

Taylor, William O. (1855 – 1923), *With Custer on the Little Bighorn: A Newly-Discovered First-Person Account.* New York: Viking, 1996.

Terrell, John Upton, *Faint the Trumpet Sounds: The Life & Trial of Major Reno.* New York: D. McKay & Co., 1966.

Tillett, Leslie, ed. *Wind on the Buffalo Grass: Native American Artist-Historians.* New York: Thomas Y. Crowell Co., 1976.

Two Hawk, Albert H. (1888 – 1975), Sicangu Lakota. Oral histories and recollections.

Vaughn, J. W., *With Crook at the Rosebud.* Harrisburg, PA: The Stackpole Co., 1st edition, 1956.

Vestal, Stanley, *Sitting Bull: Champion of the Sioux.* Boston & New York: Houghton Mifflin Co., 1932.

Wallace, George Daniel (1851 – 1890), *Letters from the Field: Wallace at the Little Big Horn.* Orange: Paragon Agency, 1997.

Welch, James, with Paul Stekler. *Killing Custer: The Battle of Little Bighorn and the Fate of the Plains Indians.* New York: W.W. Norton and Company, 1994.

Wooden Leg (1858 – 1940), interpreted by Thomas B. Marquis, *A Warrior Who Fought Custer.* Minneapolis: The Midwest Co., 1931

Maps

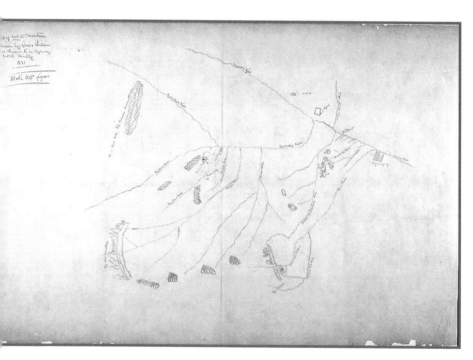

A drawing by Chief Red Horse of the battle at the Little Bighorn.
Courtesy of the Smithsonian Institute.

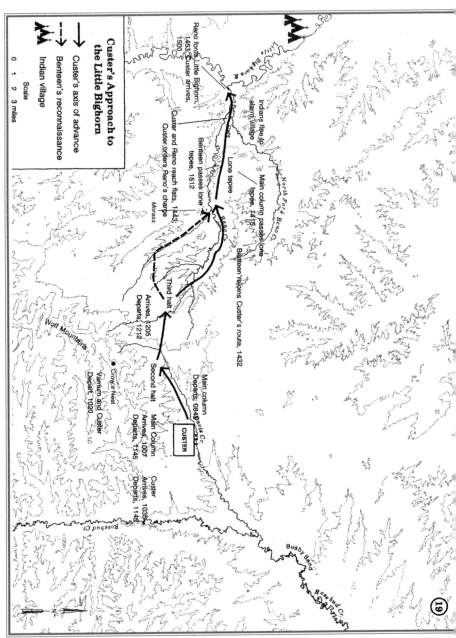

Custer's Approach to the Little Bighorn

Custer's axis of advance

Benteen's reconnaissance

Indian village

Scale
0 1 2 3 miles

Reno fords Little Bighorn,
1453; Custer arrives,
1500

Indians flee to
alarm Village

Custer and Reno reach flats, 1443;
Custer orders Reno's charge

Benteen passes lone
tepee, 1512

Lone tepee

Main column passes lone
tepee, 1415

Benteen rejoins Custer's route, 1432

Morass

Third halt

Arrives, 1205
Departs, 1212

Wolf Mountains

Crow's Nest

Varnum and Custer
Depart, 1030

Main column
Departs, 0845

Second halt

Main Column
Arrives, 1007
Departs, 1145

Custer
Arrives, 1035
Departs, 1145

CUSTER

Busby Bend

Rosebud Cr.

Rosebud Cr.

N

⑲

Map from *Atlas of the Sioux Wars*. Courtesy of the Combat Studies Institute, Fort Leavenworth, KS.

264

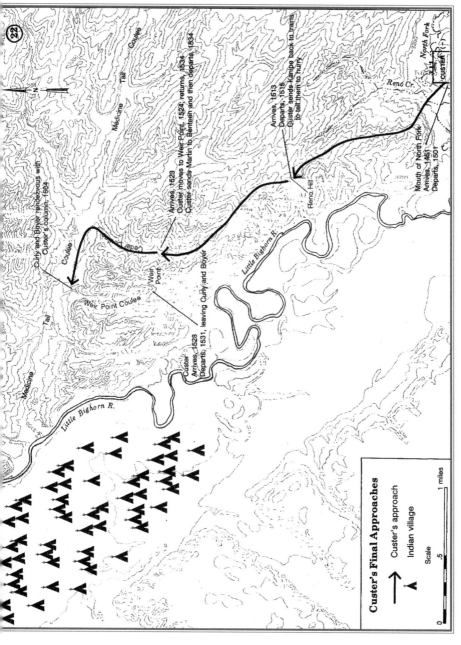

Custer's Final Approaches

→ Custer's approach

⚔ Indian village

Scale

0 .5 1 miles

Map from *Atlas of the Sioux Wars*. Courtesy of the Combat Studies Institute, Fort Leavenworth, KS.

Curly and Boyer rendezvous with Custer's column, 1604

Arrives, 1523
Custer moves to Weir Point, 1524; returns, 1634
Custer sends Martin to Benteen and then departs, 1534

Arrives, 1513
Departs, 1515
Custer sends Kanipe back to trains to tell them to hurry

Custer
Arrives, 1528
Departs, 1531, leaving Curly and Boyer

Mouth of North Fork
Arrives, 1451
Departs, 1501

Weir Point

Weir Point Coulee

Reno Hill

Reno Cr.

North Fork

CUSTER

Little Bighorn R.

Little Bighorn R.

Medicine Tail Coulee

Medicine Tail Coulee

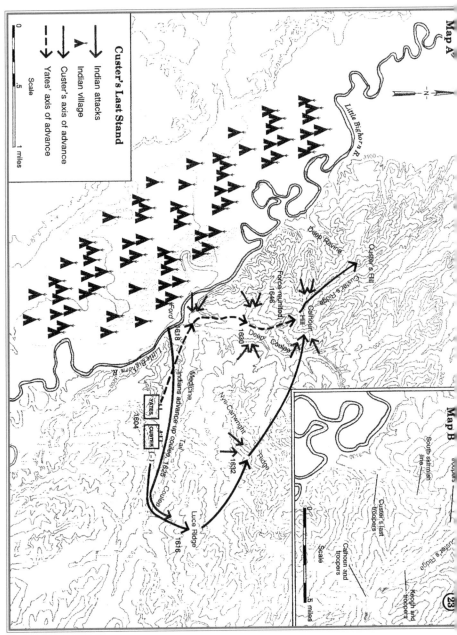

Map from *Atlas of the Sioux Wars*. Courtesy of the Combat Studies Institute, Fort Leavenworth, KS.

266

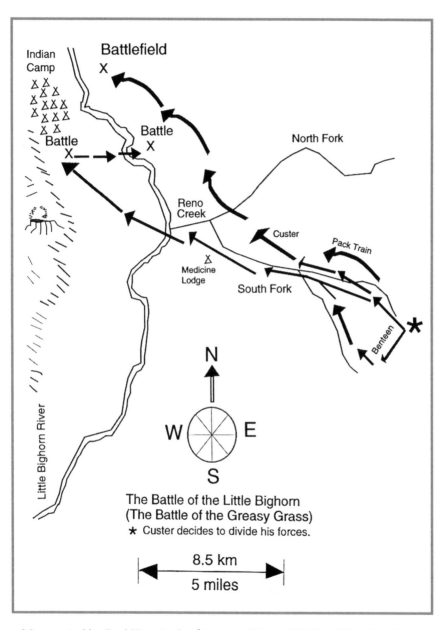

Battlefield
X

Indian
Camp

Battle
X

Battle
X

North Fork

Reno
Creek

Custer

Pack Train

Medicine
Lodge

South Fork

Benteen

★

N

W · E

S

Little Bighorn River

The Battle of the Little Bighorn
(The Battle of the Greasy Grass)
★ Custer decides to divide his forces.

8.5 km
5 miles

Map created by Paul Harwitz for this new edition of *Soldiers Falling into Camp.*

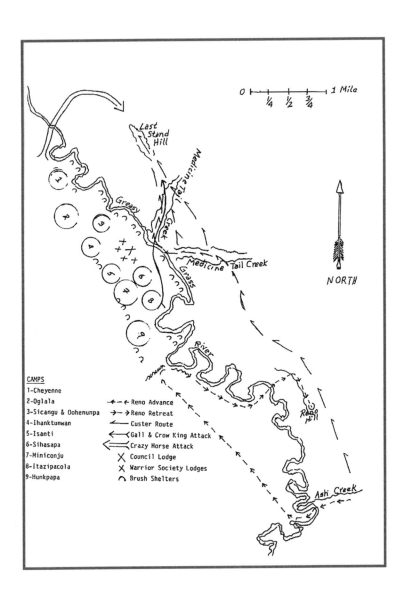

Original map source courtesy of the National Park Service.

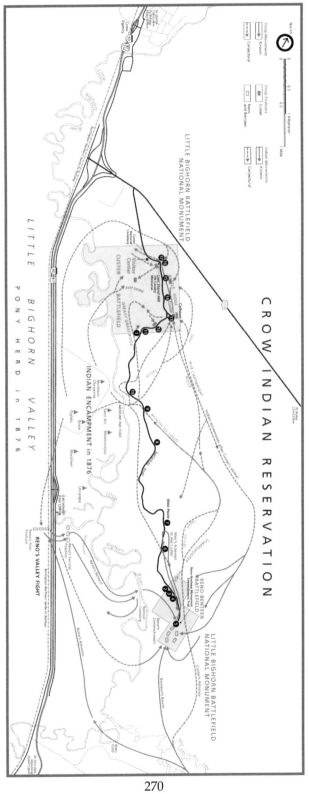

Original map source courtesy of the National Park Service.

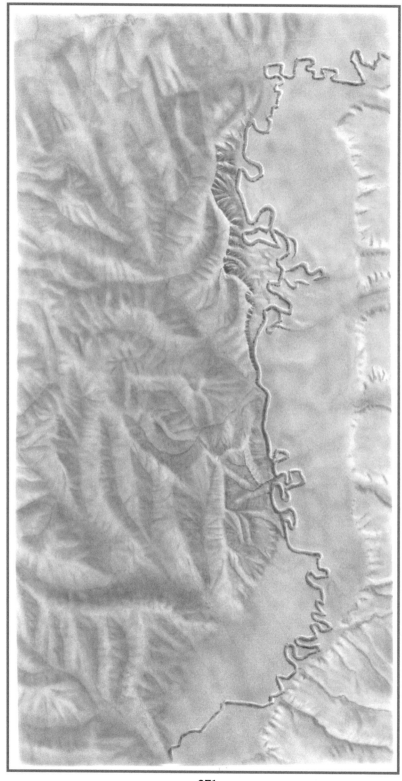

Shaded Relief Map of the Little Bighorn Original map source courtesy of the National Park Service.

Index

273